Hands Up Art Activities

Week-by-Week Projects Using Hand-Shaped Art

by Pam Campbell

illustrated by Veronica Terrill

Teaching & Learning Company

1204 Buchanan St., P.O. Box 10
Carthage, IL 62321

Cover photo by Images and More Photography

Copyright © 1995, Teaching & Learning Company

ISBN No. 1-57310-028-5

Printing No. 987654321

Teaching & Learning Company
1204 Buchanan St., P.O. Box 10
Carthage, IL 62321

TLC10028 Copyright © Teaching & Learning Company, Carthage, IL 62321

This book belongs to

_____

Table of Contents

Letter to Teacher or Parent vi
"Hand"y Ideas vii

August

Week 1: Hand in Hand Welcome the New School Year (*door decoration*) 1
Week 2: We're Busy Bees in Room 11 (*bulletin board*) 4
Week 3: Autograph Book (*take-home*) 6
Week 4: Classroom Quilt (*hall decoration*) 8

September

Week 1: Grandparents' Day (*take-home*) .10
Week 2: Bird Feeder (*outdoor*) 14
Week 3: Johnny Appleseed Day (*desk decoration*) 16
Week 4: Fall Leaves (*bulletin board/window decoration*) 19

October

Week 1: Columbus Day Ships (*take-home*) 21
Week 2: Ghost (*hall or door decoration*) .23
Week 3: Pumpkin Patch (*bulletin board*) .25
Week 4: Accomplishment (*conference material*) 27

November

Week 1: Knockout November (*door decoration*) 29
Week 2: Canoe (*bulletin board*) 30
Week 3: Turkey (*book cover*) 32
Week 4: Cornstalks (*window decoration*) .34

December

Week 1: Hanukkah Menorah (*window decoration*) 37
Week 2: Christmas Tree (*door decoration*) 40
Week 3: Kwanzaa Place Mat (*take-home*) 43
Week 4: Gift Wrap/Ornament (*take-home*) 45

January

Week 1: Super Sledders (*bulletin board*) .47
Week 2: Hands (*window decoration*) 49
Week 3: Snowflake Person (*desk decoration*) 51
Week 4: Chinese New Year Dragon (*room decoration*) 55

TLC10028 Copyright © Teaching & Learning Company, Carthage, IL 62321

February

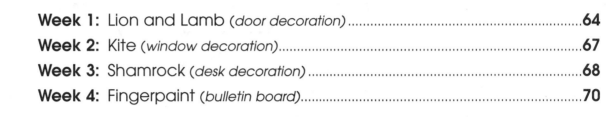

Week 1: Valentine Envelopes (*party decoration*)......................................57

Week 2: Valentine Cards (*party decoration*)..59

Week 3: Shadows (*outdoor*)..61

Week 4: Presidents' Day (*election ballot*)..62

March

Week 1: Lion and Lamb (*door decoration*)...64

Week 2: Kite (*window decoration*)..67

Week 3: Shamrock (*desk decoration*)...68

Week 4: Fingerpaint (*bulletin board*)..70

April

Week 1: Showers of Good Work (*bulletin board*)..72

Week 2: Umbrella (*desk decoration*)..74

Week 3: Eggs in Basket (*window decoration*)..76

Week 4: Tree (*hall decoration*)..79

May

Week 1: Grocery Bag Fish Piñata (*room decoration*)...................................81

Week 2: Mother's Day Gift (*take-home*)..83

Week 3: Flower (*window decoration*)..85

Week 4: Butterfly (*window decoration*)..87

Summer

Week 1: This Is a "Berry" Special Class (*door decoration*)..........................89

Week 2: Notepad for Father's Day (*take-home*)..91

Week 3: Fireworks (*bulletin board*)..93

Week 4: Splash in for a Great Summer (*bulletin board*)..............................95

General

Week 1: Happy Birthday (*desk decoration*)...97

Week 2: Get Well (*card or picture*)..100

Week 3: Welcome (*card or picture*)...102

Week 4: Thank-You (*card*)..104

Dear Teacher or Parent,

This book offers children a unique opportunity to use their own hand shapes to create weekly crafts and projects throughout the entire school year. In using their own hand shapes, your children will be able to create items as individual as themselves!

The many projects in this book use children's hand shapes to create seasonal, holiday and school-related crafts, gifts, decorations and displays. There are four weekly activities for each month. You can use one per week or pick and choose activities to fit into your own curriculum. Literature selections that relate to the topic of the activity are given for each project. The literature can be used to broaden students' knowledge and demonstrate a link between literature and learning.

For each activity, you'll find clear, easy-to-follow directions. Most activities have reproducible patterns which you can copy for as many students as needed. In some cases, you'll find simple recipes for snacks and treats that correlate to the activity. In other instances, a reproducible letter to parents or guardians has been included to request permission for a field trip or special activity.

Combining hands-on projects with hand-shaped materials gives you the best of both—the excitement and motivation that comes from the process of doing (as well as the sense of success and accomplishment when the project is completed) plus the special and memorable experience of using individual hand shapes as an integral part of the activity. Some of these projects will decorate your classroom, some of them will be used in your lessons, and some of them will find their way to your students' homes and into the hearts of parents, grandparents, other relatives and friends.

Enjoy!

Sincerely,

Pam

Pam Campbell

"Hand"y Ideas

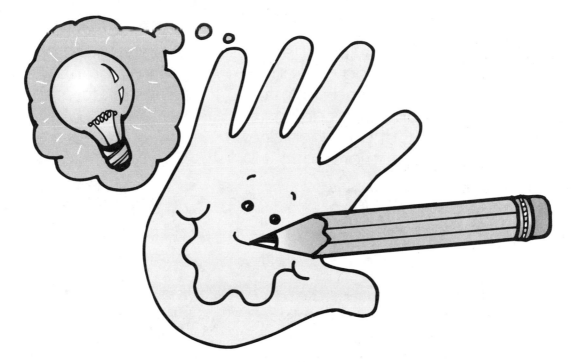

There are an infinite number of creative ideas for using children's hand shapes in arts and crafts activities. I presented many of my favorite and most successful in this book. I hope you will be encouraged to embellish and experiment with what's included here and perhaps come up with activities of your own.

- Have children work in pairs. Instead of tracing their own hand shapes, ask them to trace their partner's.

- Experiment with a variety of finger positions.

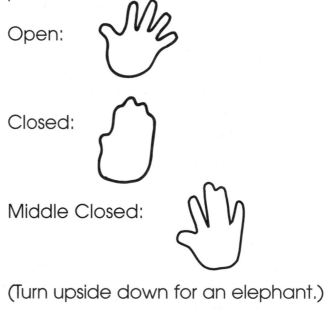

Open:

Closed:

Middle Closed:

(Turn upside down for an elephant.)

Middle Open:

(Two of these make a nice crown.)

- You could use just about any of the ideas in this book with finger-paint. Instead of tracing and cutting, paint the fingers and palms of students' hands and press down on white paper. Cut out when dry and proceed with the project.

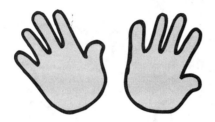

- Adapt some of the ideas in this book to use fingerpaints and print on white T-shirts (turkey, Christmas tree, gift wrap, etc.).

- Use a child's hand shape to identify his cubbie, coat hook, storage box or other personal area.

- Adapt some of the ideas in this book to make plaster of Paris tiles. (Grandparents' Day, flowers–use c craft stick to etch in the stem and leaves, etc.)

- Trace hand shapes onto 5" x 7" (13 x 18 cm) index cards. Write spelling words, math facts, numbers, alphabet letters or other information to be studied inside the outline for a personalized set of flash cards.

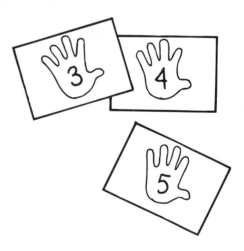

Hand in Hand Welcome the New School Year

Materials

white tagboard
red, white and blue
    construction paper
markers or crayons
scissors

Directions

Enlarge the pattern on page 2 onto white tagboard, color and cut out. Use this as the centerpiece for your door decoration. Then have students trace their open hand shapes onto red, white and blue construction paper and cut out. Use these hand shapes to circle the globe centerpiece.

Literature Selection

Timothy Goes to School
by Rosemary Wells
Dial, 1981

Selected Activity

Discuss with students why they used red, white and blue for their hand shapes. It is because we live in the United States of America and our country's flag is red, white and blue.

Use the flag on page 3 to duplicate and have students color. For younger students, the teacher may want to color a model for students to copy. Older children can copy a real flag if one is displayed in the classroom.

Use these flags to decorate your bulletin board or as covers for individual student folders. Children can collect/create material about their country to store in the folders.

Extended Activity

Research flags from other countries. Make copies of each flag for students to color appropriately.

Note

See pages 2 and 3 for patterns to be used with this activity.

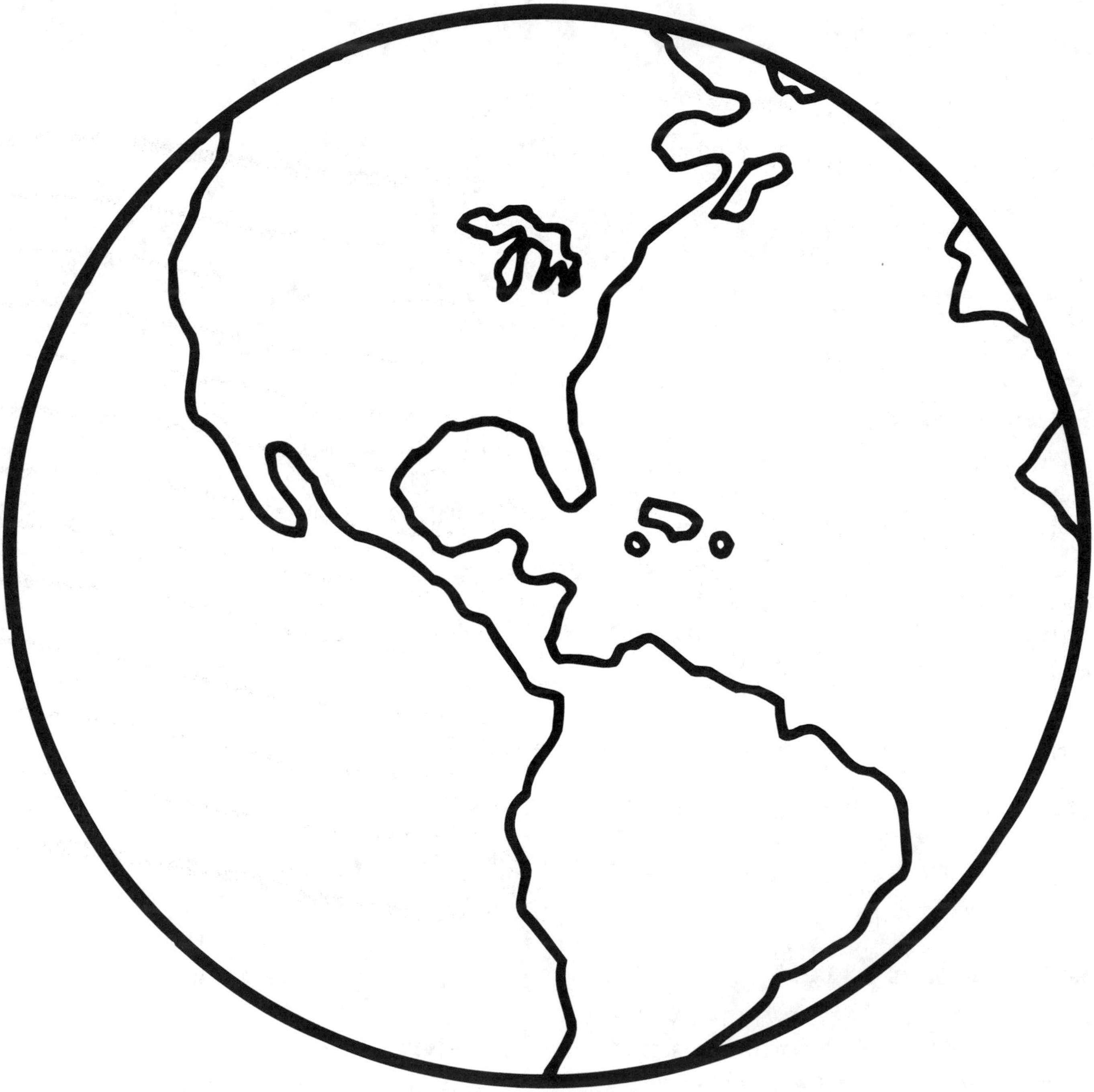

We're Busy Bees in Room 11

Materials

- white and yellow construction paper
- black, white and yellow tissue paper in 2" x 2" (5 x 5 cm) squares
- black pipe cleaners
- black and red licorice
- scissors
- glue
- pencil

Directions

Trace three closed hand shapes onto white construction paper and draw lines representing the bee's stripes on the hand shape that will represent the bee's body. Then cut out the hand shapes. Glue one hand shape on the left side of the body and the third shape on the right side of the body for the wings. Use 2" x 2" (5 x 5 cm) squares of black and yellow tissue paper for stripes on bee's body. Wrap one square of tissue paper over the eraser end of a pencil. Dip the tissue into glue and stick it onto the body of the bee. Use yellow tissue squares for one row, then black tissue squares for the next row. Continue to alternate colors with each row until the body of the bee is covered. Then use all white tissue paper squares to cover the wings. Use the pattern on page 5 to cut a head from yellow construction paper. Add black pipe cleaners for antenna. Cut small pieces of black licorice for the eyes and red licorice for the mouth. (Be sure to allow enough licorice for students to taste while working.)

Literature Selections

The Bee Tree
by Patricia Polacco
Philomel Books, 1993

The Honeybee and the Robber
by Eric Carle
Scholastic, Inc., 1994

Selected Activity

Add a beehive made from tan tagboard and decorate. For a 3-D effect, add small wire craft bees.

Note

See page 5 for patterns to be used with this activity.

Autograph Book

Materials

white or colored typing paper
colored construction paper
scissors
stapler
pencil
markers

Directions

Trace hand shape onto white or colored typing paper. Then cut several sheets at a time, until each student has enough hand shapes for every child and teacher in the class. It works nicely if every student has her own color of typing paper to use. Students should sign their first and last names onto each hand shape and include a personal message, if desired, to give to every classmate and teacher in the class. When the hand shapes have all been distributed, each child and teacher can make a book cover by tracing his own hand shape two times onto construction paper. Then cut out the shapes. Write a title on the construction paper hand shape used as the front cover. Use the other construction paper hand shape for the back cover. Staple the individual, autographed hand shapes between the front and back covers to make a book. This will help students learn their classmates' names and how to spell each name. It is also helpful for parents to learn who is in their child's class.

Literature Selections

Anna Banana and Me
by Lenore Blegvad
Macmillan, 1985

Frog and Toad Are Friends
by Arnold Lobel
Harper & Row, 1970

These books stress the importance of friendship and accepting friends as they are.

Selected Activity

Use colored chalk to sign autographs and write positive messages on the school sidewalk or cement play area for other classes to read.

Classroom Quilt

Materials

construction paper squares in
   your school colors
yarn
scissors
tape
glue
pencil

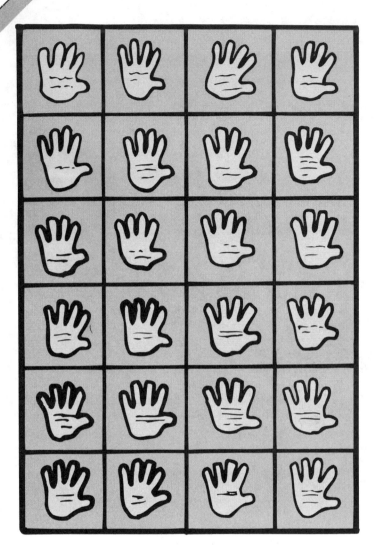

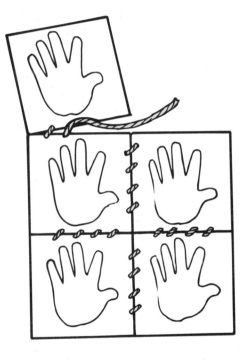

Directions

Students should trace their open hand shape onto construction paper that matches one of your school colors and cut out. Use the lighter school color for the hand shapes and the darker school color as the quilt block background. On each hand shape, students should draw or write about what they like best about school. When the hand shapes are finished, glue them onto sheets of construction paper to make quilt blocks. When all the quilt blocks are made, use yarn or tape to join the blocks together to make a paper quilt. Display the quilt in the classroom or hallway for others to see what your students like most about school. (If necessary, use blank blocks to make your quilt come out even.)

TLC10028 Copyright © Teaching & Learning Company, Carthage, IL 62321

Literature Selection

The Quilt Story
by Tony Johnston
illustrated by Tomie de Paola
Putnam Publishing Group, 1992

Selected Activities

Have a Blanket/Quilt Day at your school. Use the letter below to send home to parents so they will know to send a blanket/quilt to school. On Blanket/Quilt Day, students spend the whole day on the floor with their blanket/quilt. Plan lots of floor activities and stories. Guest readers are nice on this day, too. Allow students to tell about their blanket or quilt and what makes it special to them.

Dear Parents:

Our class will be celebrating Blanket/Quilt Day on _____.

Please allow your child to bring his/her favorite blanket/quilt to school on this day. We will be discussing why your child's blanket/quilt is special. If you feel there is something we should know about this special blanket/quilt, please send a note along with it. We invite you to visit our classroom to see the special quilt made by our class. On our quilt, we have included pictures/words to show what we like best about school. The blanket/quilt your child brings to school will be returned home on the same day. If you would like to send the blanket/quilt in a plastic bag, we will see that it is returned in the same protective bag.

Thank you,

_____

Grandparents' Day

Materials
white drawing paper
pen/pencil

Here are my hands,
They write you these lines.
I want you to know,
You are one of a kind.
Happy Grandparents Day!
Love, Kellie ♥

Directions
On a sheet of white drawing paper students trace and label their left and right hands. Under the handprints students copy this poem in their best handwriting:

> Here are my hands,
> They write you these lines.
> I want you to know,
> You are one of a kind.
> Happy Grandparents' Day!
> Love,

Literature Selection
A Visit to Grandma's
by Nancy L. Carlson
Viking, 1991

Selected Activities
Before Grandparents' Day, students may visit the local post office to mail letters to their grandparents or an elderly friend. Make prior arrangements with the postmaster so students can tour the post office and cancel their own letters, if permitted.

Extended Activity

Involve the entire school by having a Grandparents' Day luncheon. Students can invite their grandparents or an elderly friend to eat lunch with them at school. This will take a lot of preparation and planning with the lunchroom personnel, so plan early.

Note

See pages 12 and 13 for permission slips to go to the post office and the letter for grandparents.

Date: _____

Dear Parents,

We are planning a trip on _____ to the local post office to mail letters to grandparents. Please send a stamped/addressed envelope with your child to school before _____. The envelope needs to be addressed to a grandparent(s) or an elderly friend. Be sure to include your child's name/address as the return address.

Thank you,

_____

_____ has my permission to go
to the post office with his/her class on
_____.

_____

signature

Date: _____

Dear_____,

Our class went to the post office to mail this letter to you. We hope you will take the time to write back to us at school. We would love to get the mail.

Our school address is:

_____

_____

_____

_____

Attn:

_____

Thank you,

_____

13

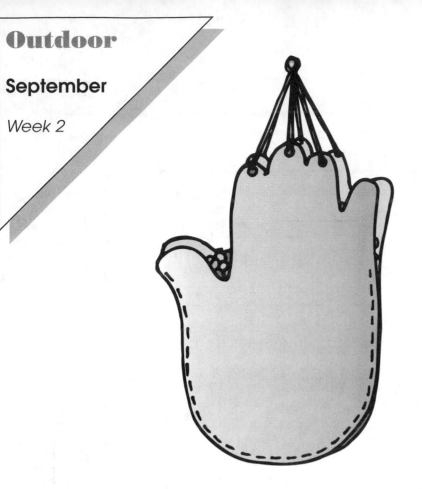
Bird Feeder

Materials

tagboard or heavy construction paper

waxed paper or clear self-adhesive paper

yarn

scissors

tape or stapler

pencil

Directions

Trace closed hands onto tagboard or heavy construction paper. Line the outside/inside hands with waxed paper, cover with clear self-adhesive paper or laminate. Connect the bottom/sides with heavy tape or staples. Leave the top open and hang with yarn. Then fill with birdseed, popcorn, bread crumbs, old cereal, raisins, etc., and hang from a tree branch on the school yard or at home.

Literature Selections

Crinkleroot's Guide to Knowing the Birds
by Jim Arnosky
Bradbury Press (Macmillan), 1992

Crinkleroot's 25 Birds Every Child Should Know
by Jim Arnosky
Bradbury Press (Macmillan), 1993

Our Yard Is Full of Birds
by Anne Rockwell
Macmillan, 1992

Suggested Activity

Research birds' coloring and markings. Display bird pictures. Have students color the bird pictures on the next page using appropriate coloring and markings.

Note

See page 15 for patterns to be used with this activity.

Johnny Appleseed Day

Materials

brown tagboard or
construction paper

crayons or markers

scissors

tape

glue

Directions

Trace two closed hand shapes onto brown tagboard or construction paper. (If using tagboard, small children may need extra help.) The thumbs need to be facing upward when tracing, to represent the basket's handle extension. Then cut out. Cut out a handle. (See pattern on page 18.) Glue at fingers of hand shapes for basket. Glue on handle at thumbs. Students can draw woven designs on baskets, if desired. Duplicate the apples on page 18 and give each student a sheet of apples to color and cut out. Glue the apples into the hand-shaped basket. Then tape the basket of apples to the front of each child's desk.

Literature Selection

Johnny Appleseed
by Steven Kellogg
Morrow Jr. Books, 1988

Prior to making the hand-shaped baskets of apples, read and discuss Johnny Appleseed's adventures.

16

Suggested Activity

After the baskets are made, reward students for their hard work with a caramel apple snack.

Caramel Dip

1 8 oz. pkg. (224 g) cream cheese

1 cup (240 ml) brown sugar

3 T. (45 ml) sugar

1 tsp. (5 ml) vanilla

Soften cream cheese then stir in remaining ingredients. Be sure to mix well. Do not use electric mixer.

Cut apple slices and dip. (Students who may not like the caramel dip can eat apple slices plain.)

Note

See page 18 for patterns to be used with this activity.

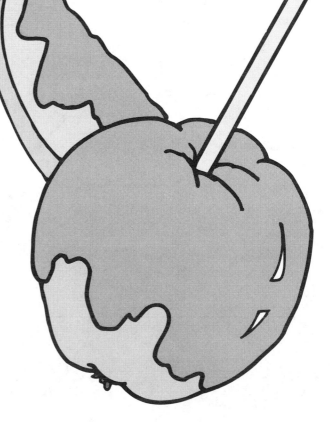

Fall Leaves

Materials

construction paper in fall colors
black marker
tempera paint
sponges
pencils

Discovering Trees
by Keith Brandt
Troll Associates, 1982

Directions

Trace hands onto construction paper of various fall colors. Draw lines with a heavy black marker to represent veins in leaves. Then sponge-paint fall colors onto the front of the leaf handprints.

Optional: When the front is dry, turn the leaf over and sponge-paint the back.

Use the leaves to decorate classroom windows or on a bulletin board with a large tree (pattern on page 20) made from brown and green bulletin board paper. The bulletin board title could read: "You Will 'Fall' for Us."

Suggested Activity

Prior to making hand-shaped leaves, take students on a nature walk to collect fallen leaves. During the walk discuss leaf shapes, colors, veins, stems, etc. This will help students know more about how their own hand-shaped leaves should look when they are finished.

Note

See page 20 for tree pattern to be enlarged and used with this activity.

Literature Selections

The Tree
by Gallimard Jeunesse and
    Pascale de Bourgoing
First Discovery Book–Scholastic, Inc., 1992

Columbus Day Ships

Materials

half-pint milk cartons

brown construction
  paper

off-white construction
  paper

craft sticks

scissors

glue

tape

Directions
For Making Ships:

Rinse out an empty half-pint milk cartons and let dry. Then tape down the end that has been opened and make a rectangular three-dimensional box. Cover this box with brown construction paper which has been cut to fit around the box.

Optional: Cover the end of the box with brown construction paper, too.

Help students label their ships by writing *Nina, Pinta* and *Santa Maria* on the chalkboard for students to copy.

For Making Hand-Shaped Sails:

Trace a closed handprint onto off-white construction paper and cut out. Glue the handprint onto a craft stick. Then poke the craft stick down into the milk carton ship.

Optional: Use tape and put the hand-shaped sail onto a thin straw. The sail will move more freely on the straw.

Literature Selections

Christopher Columbus
by Ann McGovern
Scholastic, Inc., 1992

In Fourteen Ninety-Two
by Jean Marzollo
Scholastic, Inc., 1991

These books will familiarize children with Christopher Columbus and why he is famous.

Note

If you want to make a bulletin board display showing boats with hand-shaped sails, see page 22 for pattern.

*Attach sails here.

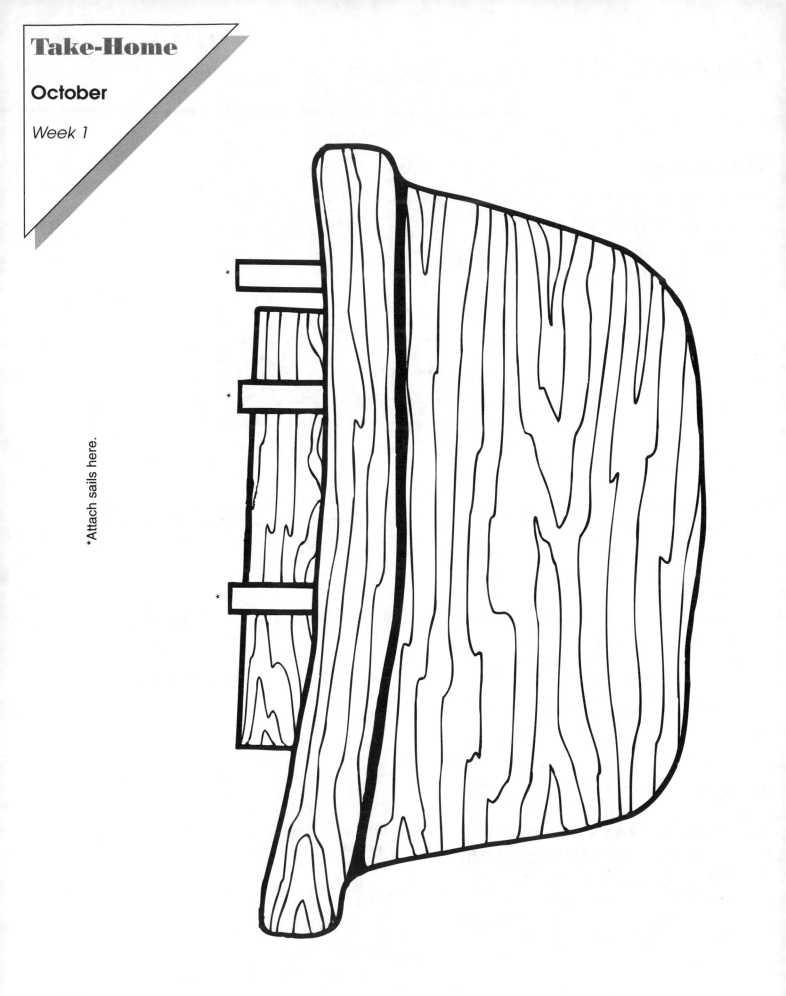

Ghost

Materials

white paint
black construction paper
3-D wiggly eyes
small pom-poms
string licorice
glue

Directions

Put entire hand into white paint. Press palm of hand firmly onto black construction paper. Then sweep the fingers to fan out the bottom of ghost. Add three-dimensional wiggly eyes, pom-pom nose and string licorice mouth. These ghosts also look nice on purple construction paper. Be sure to put the artist's name on the front of the picture so parents can determine which picture belongs to their child when they visit the school for first quarter conferences.

Optional: The ghosts can also be used as part of a Halloween picture.

For Making a Halloween Night Scene:

Use a large sheet of tagboard for the background. Then draw a Halloween scene with white or yellow crayon on the tagboard. After the scene is drawn, paint over the entire tagboard with black watercolors. The wax from the crayon will allow the scene to show through the black watercolors. When the paint dries, cut out the hand-shaped ghost and glue it into the scene to create a three-dimensional effect.

Literature Selections

Best Halloween Book
by Patricia Whitehead
Troll Associates, 1985

Georgie and the Robbers
by Robert Bright
Doubleday & Co. Inc., 1963

Note

See page 24 for suggested scenes to be used with this activity.

Suggested Scenes to Draw on Tagboard

Pumpkin Patch

Materials

orange balloons

black marker

green construction paper or tagboard

white and black construction paper

scissors

Picking Apples & Pumpkins
by Amy and Richard Hutchings
Scholastic, Inc., 1994

Directions

Blow up one orange balloon for each student and tie closed.

Optional: Draw black lines on each balloon to make it look more like a pumpkin.

Trace two closed handprints onto green construction paper or tagboard. Cut out the handprints and poke a hole in the palms. Slip the tied end of the balloon through the holes in each handprint to make leaves for the pumpkin. Use the pumpkins to make a pumpkin patch for an October bulletin board. Add a fence on a black background with a bright white full moon.

Literature Selections

The Little Old Lady Who Was Not Afraid of Anything
by Linda Williams
Crowell Jr., 1986

Suggested Activity

Carve a real pumpkin with your students to make a jack-o'-lantern for your classroom. After cleaning out the pumpkin, ask students to predict/record how many pumpkin seeds they think came out of the pumpkin. Then count them together, and check the recorded predictions. After counting the seeds, clean them and put on a cookie sheet to bake and eat later.

Note

See page 26 for patterns to be used with this activity.

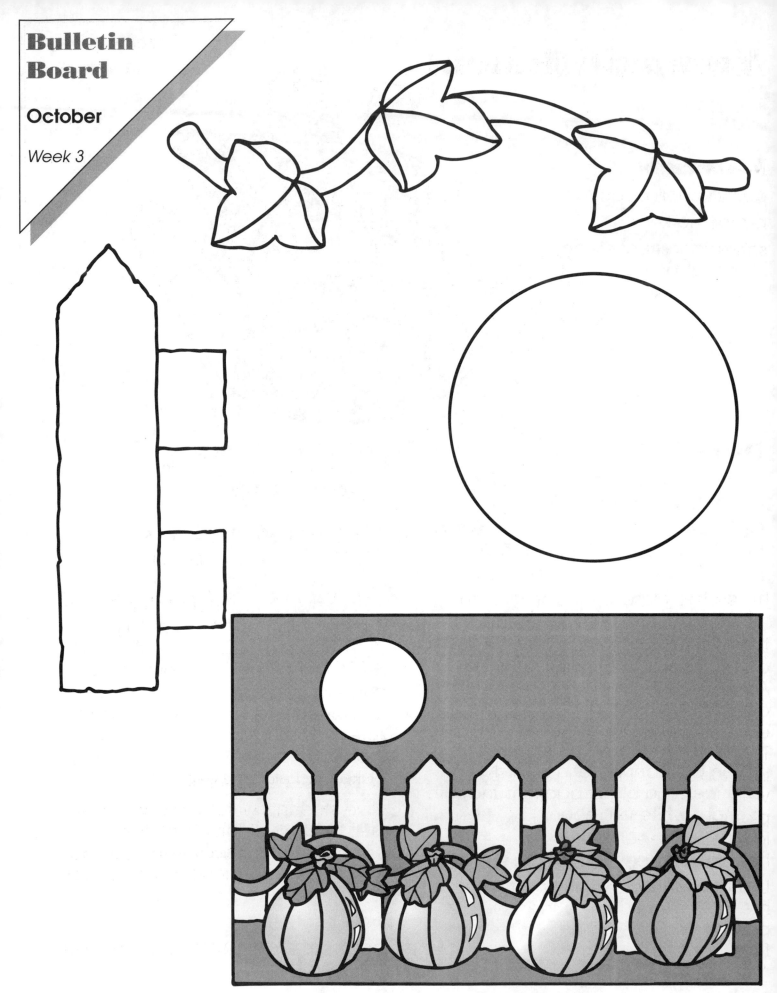

Accomplishment

Materials

construction paper
pencil
scissors

Directions

Trace open handprint (exaggerating the size) onto large, brightly colored construction paper and cut out. Add a face on the palm section, if desired. Have students number each finger/thumb area as shown. Then students should write one thing in each area that they feel they do well. Ask younger children to find pictures in magazines or draw their ideas. The teacher or teacher's helper can label each idea.

Use these hand-shaped accomplishments to share positive ideas with parents during parent/teacher conferences.

Literature Selections

Luckiest One of All
by Bill Peet
Houghton-Mifflin, 1982

All I Am
by Eileen Roe
Bradbury Press, 1992

Self-Assessment

Have students write or draw a picture to tell what they think the teacher should discuss with their parents at parent/teacher conferences.

Note

See page 28 for patterns to be used with this activity.

See What I Can Do!

_____

name

Paste
hand shape
here.

Knockout November

Materials

construction paper

glitter glue

pencil

decorative items (sequins,
  ribbon, star stickers, etc.)

Directions

Trace closed hand shapes onto brightly colored construction paper. To make the shape of a boxing glove, do not trace around each finger. Cut out. Using glitter glue, write student's first name on one glove and last name on the other glove. Then decorate the gloves using glitter, sequins, ribbon, star stickers, etc.

Literature Selection

On Market Street
by Arnold Lobel
Greenwillow, 1981

Suggested Activities

Use the boxing gloves with names printed on them to learn more about each other's names.

For example:

- Count the letters in each person's first name, then graph the results. Discuss whose name has the most letters, least letters, same number of letters, etc.

- Count the letters in each person's last name and repeat the above activity.

- Count the letters in each person's first and last names together and repeat the first activity.

- Discuss and count vowels and consonants in each name. Note the importance of a vowel in every word.

- Break down compound words and print onto pairs of gloves.

- Print spelling words on the gloves.

- Print antonyms or synonyms on pairs of gloves.

Canoe

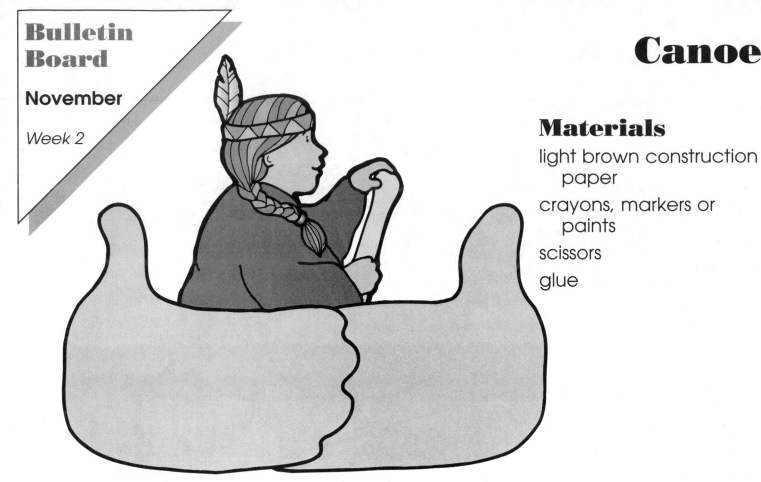

Materials

light brown construction paper

crayons, markers or paints

scissors

glue

Directions

Trace closed hand shapes onto light brown construction paper with thumbs straight up. Cut out hand shapes, then glue them together with fingers slightly overlapping as shown. Be sure to paint brightly colored designs on the sides of each hand-shaped canoe. Color and cut out the Indian patterns on page 31 to put in the canoe.

Literature Selections

Drawing America: The Story of the First Thanksgiving
by Elaine Raphael and Don Bolognese
Scholastic, Inc., 1991

'Twas the Night Before Thanksgiving
by Dave Pilkey
Orchard Books Watts, 1990

The Thanksgiving Story
by Alice Dalgliesh
Aladdin (Macmillan), 1985

Suggested Activity

Introduce this activity with a discussion about how the Indians helped the Pilgrims and why the United States celebrates Thanksgiving. After discussing the first Thanksgiving feast, make your own classroom Thanksgiving feast. Wear Indian hats, vests and beads; Pilgrim hats, capes and collars. Eat foods which are harvested in your area.

Note

See page 31 for patterns to be used with this activity.

30

Turkey

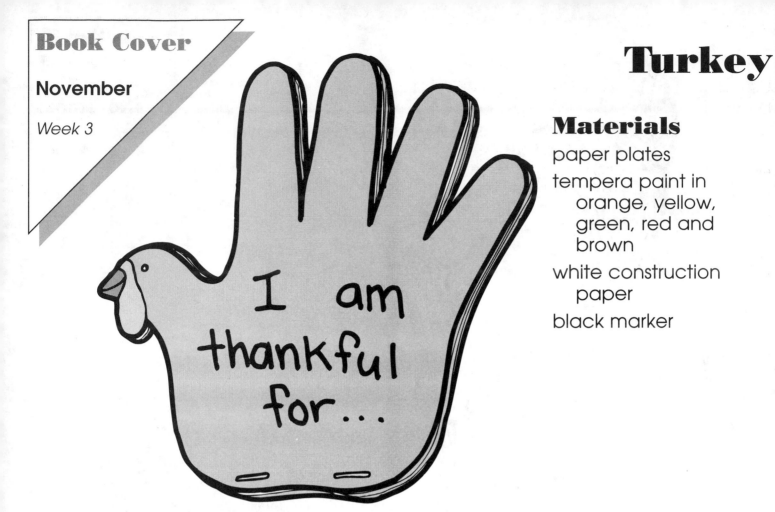

Materials

paper plates

tempera paint in orange, yellow, green, red and brown

white construction paper

black marker

Suggested Activity

Make a three- to five-page book and use the hand-shaped turkey for a cover.

Book Topics

Things I am thankful for . . .
Use one idea per page with illustrations.

What I like to eat for Thanksgiving dinner . . .
Use one idea per page with illustrations.

My family (I am thankful for my family) . . .
Use one family member per page with illustrations.

I am thankful because I can do . . .
Use one task per page with illustrations.

Literature Selections

N.C. Wyeth's Pilgrims
by Robert San Souci
Chronicle Books, 1991

Sarah Morton's Day
by Kate Waters
Scholastic, Inc., 1989

Directions

Use orange, yellow, green, red and brown paint. Have the paint arranged on paper plates as shown, so students can put one finger in each color and the palm of their hand in brown. When the paint is on each finger and palm, lay hand onto white construction paper to make hand-shaped turkey. With black marker add eye, beak, wattle and feet.

Optional: Instead of using marker, add wiggly eyes and red felt for wattle.

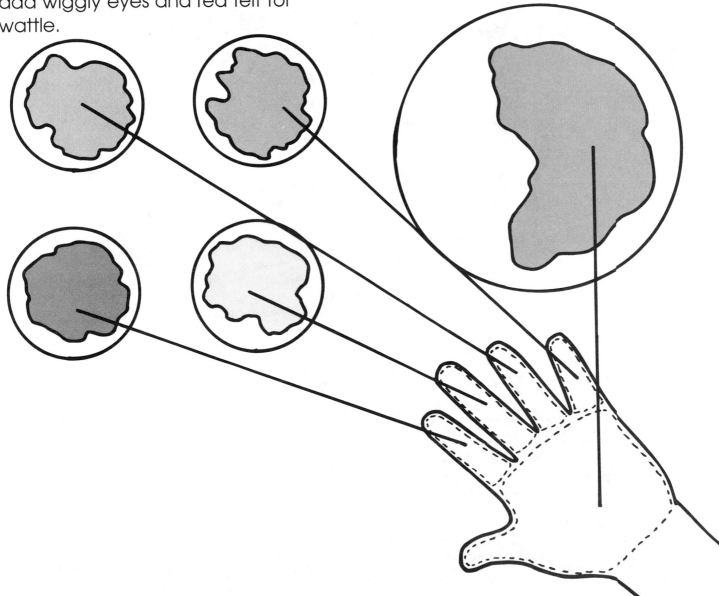

Window Decoration

November

Week 4

Cornstalks

Materials

yellow construction paper

black, light brown and green marker or crayon

scissors

glue

pencil

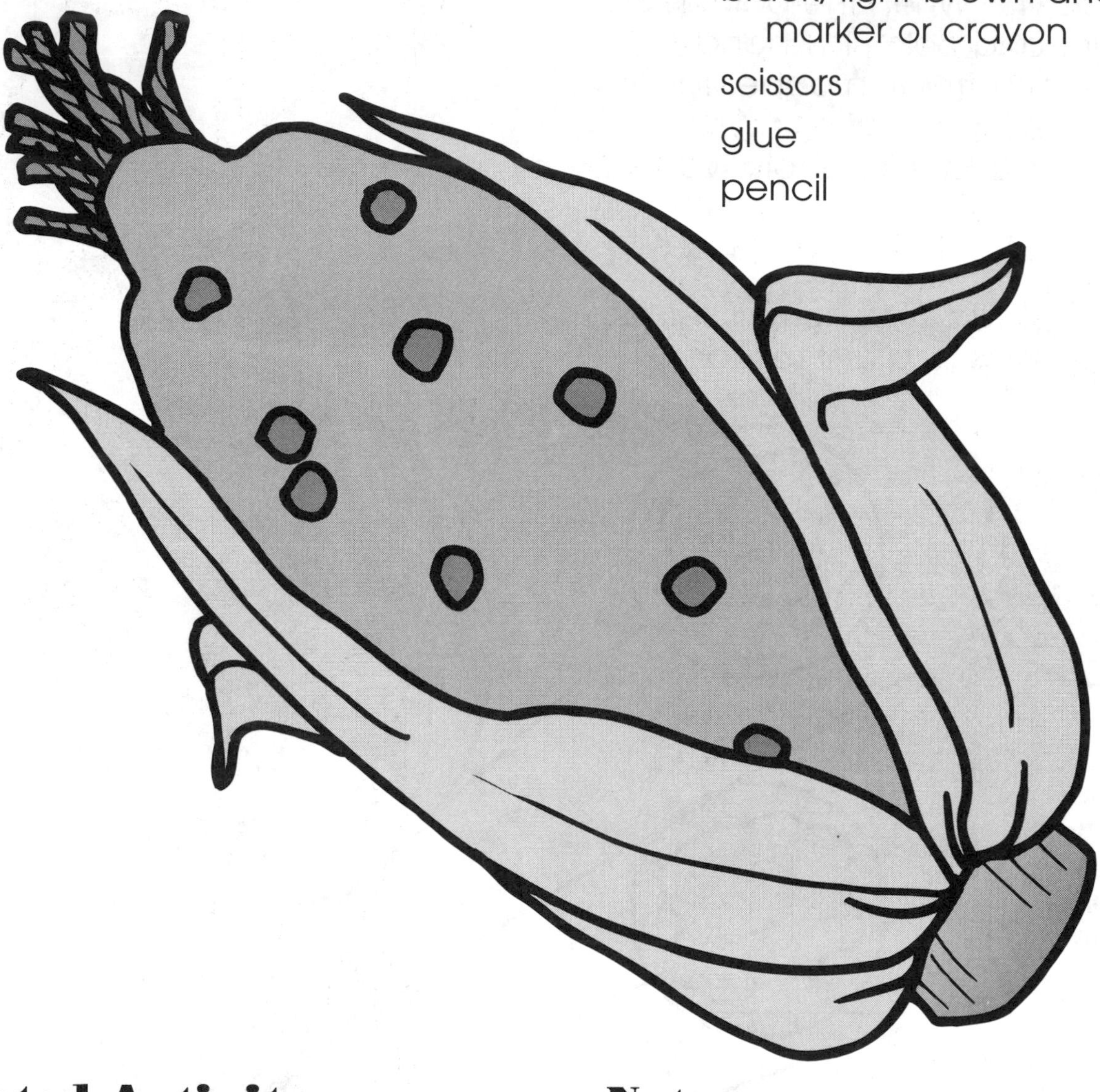

Selected Activity

Tour a cornfield (if there is one near your school) to examine the stalks, husks and ears of corn. If there is not a cornfield nearby, maybe you can find a garden with cornstalks to examine. Bring corn on the cob to school, shuck the husks, clean, cook and eat the corn on the cob at school.

Note

See page 36 for patterns to be used with this activity.

Directions

Trace three closed hand shapes onto yellow construction paper to make the ears of corn. (Optional: Use black crayon or marker to make small circles on each hand shape to represent corn kernels.) Reproduce the patterns on page 36 to make cornstalks and husks. Stalks should be colored a light brown and corn husks can be green (if the corn is not ready for harvest) or light brown (if the corn is ready to be harvested). Glue the hand-shaped ears of corn into the husks. Then glue the corn and husks to the stalk.

These cornstalks look especially nice growing in your window. If you prefer, you can plant them on your bulletin board, along the walls of your classroom or in the hallway. Perhaps your cafeteria could use a little decorating? What about a local business? (Grocery store windows make excellent cornfields!)

Literature Selections

Corn Is Maize: The Gift of the Indians
by Aliki
Crowell Jr. Books, 1976

Corn: What It Is, What It Does
by Cynthia Kellogg
Greenwillow, 1989

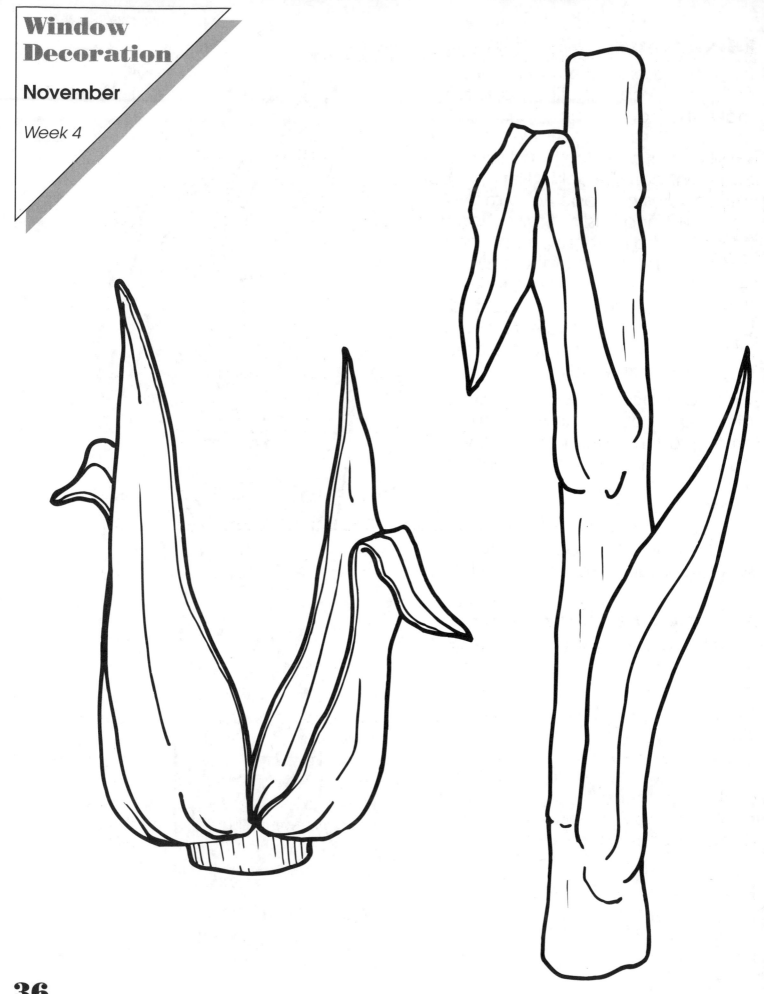

Hanukkah Menorah

Materials

brightly colored construction paper

yellow or orange tissue
paper

scissors

glue

pencil

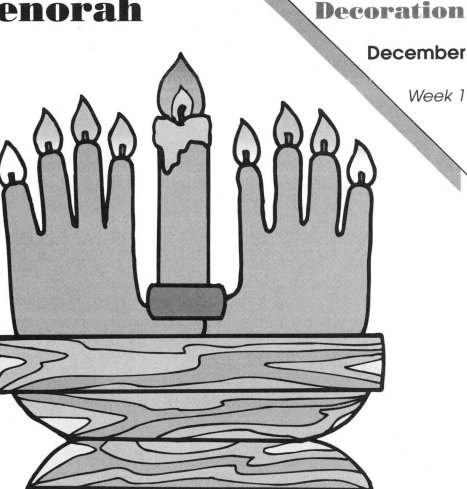

Directions

Trace both hands onto brightly colored construction paper, making
sure the thumbs are well-separated
from the fingers. Then cut out. Glue
the thumb sections of hand shapes
to the large candle pattern on page
38. Add yellow or orange tissue
paper flames to the candles for
each day of Hanukkah. Copy, color
and cut out the candle holder (pattern on page 39). Glue it over the
bottom of the candles as shown.

Literature Selections

My First Chanukah
by Tomie de Paola
Putnam, 1989

*A Great Miracle Happened There:
A Chanukah Story*
by Karla Kuskin
HarperCollins, 1993

Suggested Activity

Prior to making the hand-shaped
menorah, introduce background
information about Hanukkah and
Jewish traditions. Discuss the Jewish
dreidel toy. Try to find a menorah,
make one or have a picture of one
to show the children while they
make their own hand-shaped
menorah.

Note

See pages 38 and 39 for patterns to
be used with this activity.

37

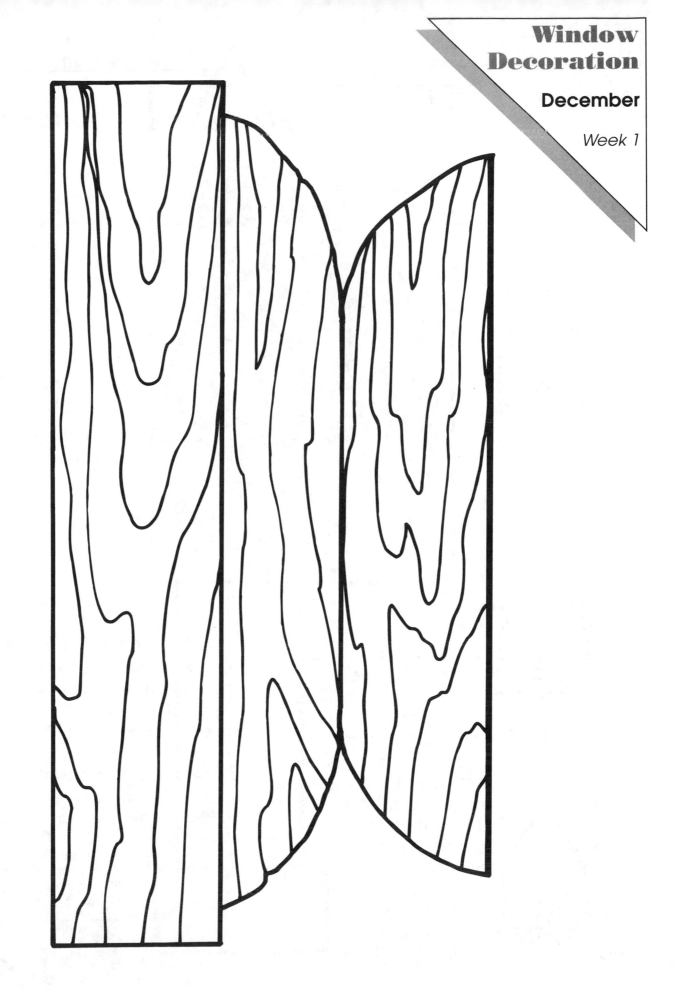

Christmas Tree

Materials

sponges (one for each child)

paper plates

dark green tempera paint

red bulletin board paper

holiday stickers

pencil

construction paper in school colors

markers

tape

Directions

Help each child trace a closed hand shape onto a piece of sponge. Be sure to write the child's name on the hand-shaped sponge. Then cut out the sponge patterns for students to use to paint a large Christmas tree on red bulletin board paper. Outline a simple tree shape on the paper for students to use when painting. Place a small amount of green tempera paint on a paper plate. Dip hand-shaped sponge into paint, then press onto paper. Use the trunk pattern on page 42 to make the bottom of the tree. Cut out and tape on the bulletin board paper.

Note: Do not soak the sponge in the paint–a light print is much more effective. Add stickers for ornaments when the paint is dry. Enlarge the pattern on page 42 to make a tree skirt. Allow students to help color the tree skirt with markers.

Literature Selection

Santa's Favorite Story
by Hisako Aoki and Ivan Gantschev
Scholastic, Inc., 1991

40

Suggested Activity

Use one of the recipes below to create ornaments for your tree. Either recipe will make ceramic-like decorations which your children can take home and enjoy for many years.

Please Note: While there is nothing harmful in any of the ingredients, these ornaments are NOT to be eaten.

When dry, the ornaments can be colored with paints or markers, or decorated with glitter, sequins, buttons, ribbon, lace, etc.

Cook's Clay Cookies

4 cups (960 ml) flour

1 cup. (240 ml) salt

1¹/₂ cups (360 ml) water

Combine flour and salt. Gradually add water. Knead for five minutes to blend thoroughly. Roll out to ¹/₄" (.6 cm) thickness; cut with floured cookie cutter. Pierce with drinking straw to create a hole for hanging. Bake on ungreased cookie sheet at 325°F (160°C) until light brown, about 30 minutes, or air dry on a rack for 48 hours.

China Cookies

1 cup (240 ml) cornstarch

2 cups (480 ml) baking soda

1¹/₄ cups (300 ml) water

Combine cornstarch and soda in a saucepan. Gradually add water. Heat, stirring constantly, until mixture is the consistency of moist mashed potatoes. Turn onto plate; cover with a damp towel. Knead when cool enough to handle. Roll out to ¹/₄" (.6 cm) thickness; cut with cookie cutters. Pierce with drinking straw to create a hole for hanging. Air dry on rack several days.

Note

See page 42 for the tree skirt and tree trunk patterns to be used with this activity.

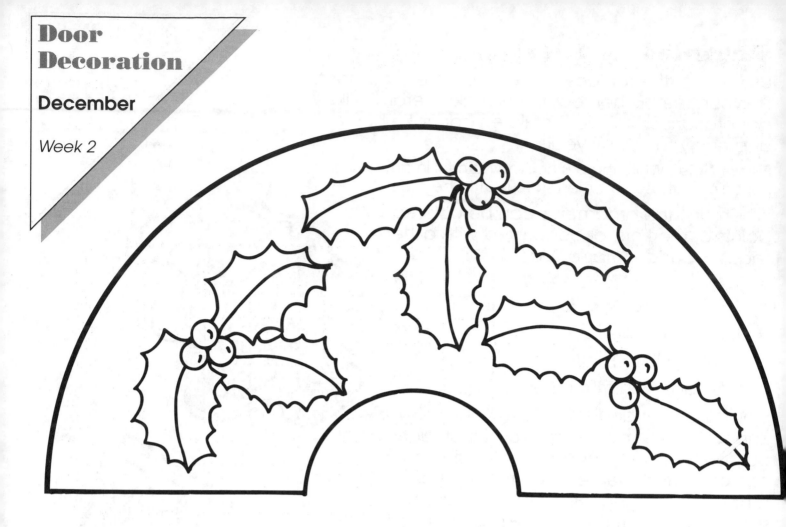

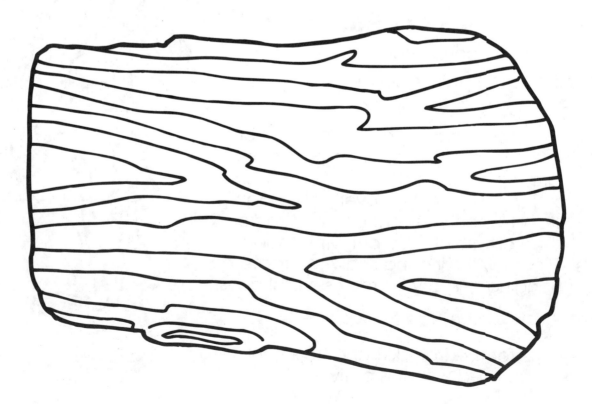

Kwanzaa Place Mat

Materials

11" x 14" (28 x 35 cm) construction
    paper
1" (2.5 cm) wide by 14" (35 cm) long
scissors
glue
pencil

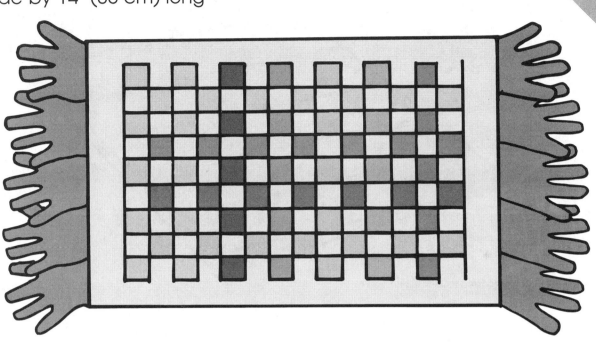

Literature Selection

Kwanzaa
by Deborah M. Chocolate
Children's, 1990

Suggested Activity

Cover the place mats with clear self-
adhesive paper or laminate for use
with real food. Use the place mats in
the cafeteria at lunchtime. This will
promote many questions from
students in other classes. Therefore,
prepare your students to be able to
explain the Kwanzaa holiday to
others. Allow students to take place
mats home to use and explain the
Kwanzaa holiday to family members.

Extended Activity

Have a Kwanzaa feast in your classroom. Bring in fruits and vegetables
and use place mats and candles to
celebrate Kwanzaa.

Directions

Use a large 11" x 14" (28 x 35 cm) piece of construction paper for the base of the place mat. Fold the paper in half and cut slits 1" (2.5 cm) wide from fold to open end but not completely to the edge. Open the paper and weave 1" (2.5 cm) wide x 14" (35 cm) long strips of various colors of construction paper over and under these slits, and glue the ends in place. This will make the place mat appear woven. Now trace several hand shapes onto one color of construction paper and cut out. These can be glued to the underside of each end of the place mat to represent fringe.

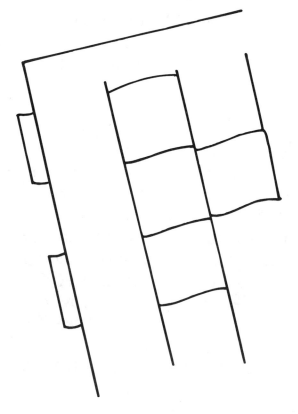

Gift Wrap

Materials

white butcher paper or lightly
   colored bulletin board paper

markers or crayons

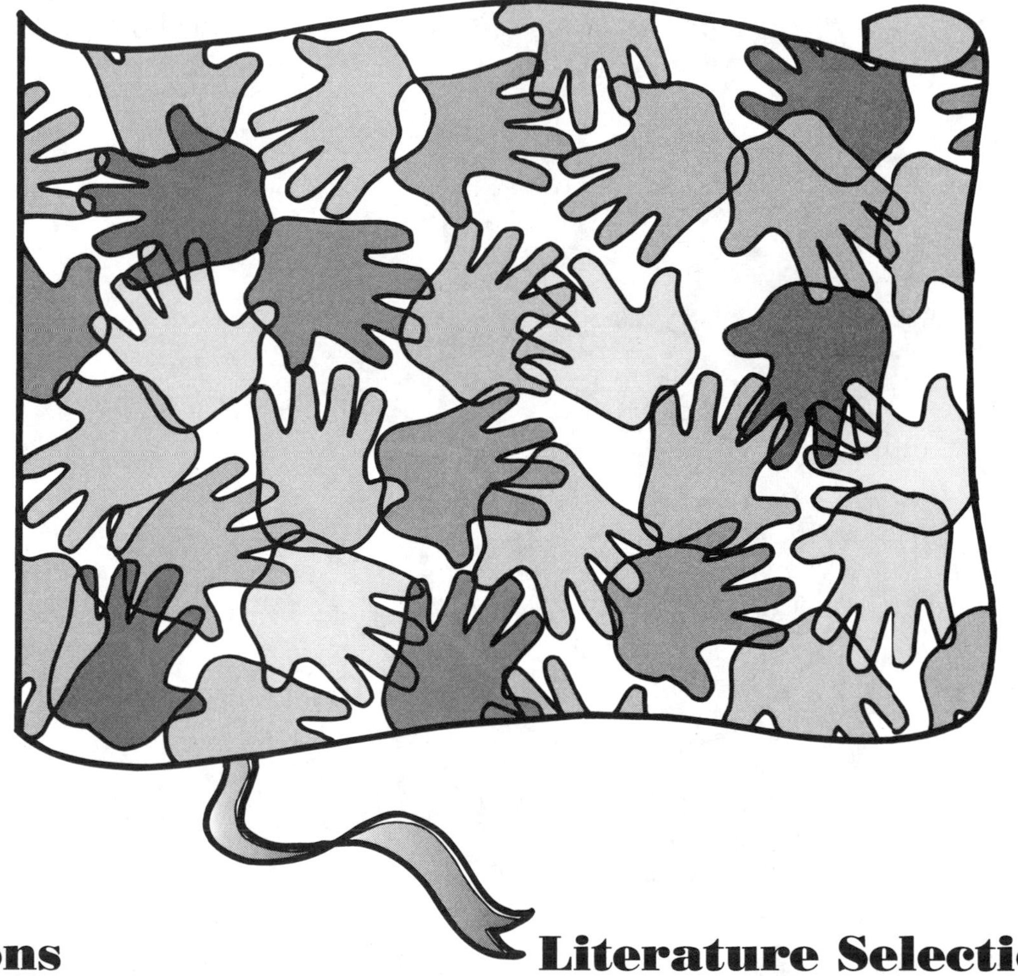

Directions

Use a 20" x 24" (51 x 61 cm) sheet of
white butcher paper or lightly colored bulletin board paper for students to trace their handprints several times in all directions, until the
entire paper is covered on one side.
With markers or crayons, students
can color all of their handprints.
After the paper is completely decorated and colored, use it to wrap the
gift that students have made for
their parents as a holiday present.

Literature Selection

Santa's Secret Helper
by Andrew Clements
Picture Book Studio, 1991

Note

See page 46 for parent gift idea.

Ornament

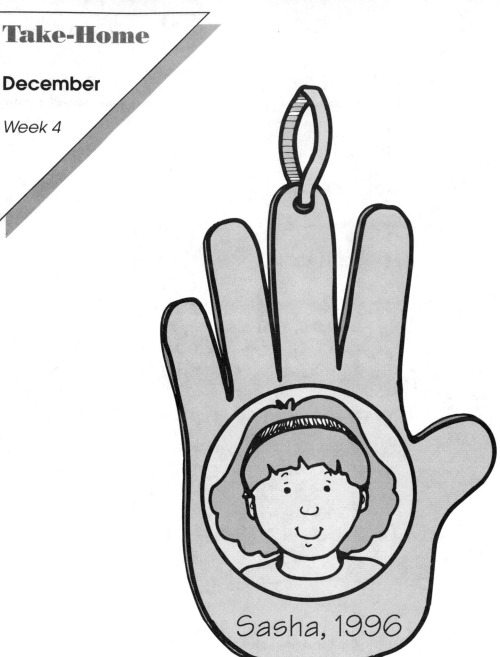

Sasha, 1996

Materials

brightly colored
   construction paper

child's photograph

pencil

scissors

glue

Suggested Activity

A gift that students can make quickly and easily for their parents is a hand-shaped ornament to hang on the Christmas tree at home.

Directions

Students trace their open hand shape onto brightly colored construction paper that has been folded in half. Then cut out the hand shape. There should be two hand shapes of identical shape and size. On one of the hand shapes, cut out a circle large enough to show a picture of the child. Then glue the two hand shapes together with the child's photo between them. Add string and an ornament hook at the top of the tallest finger. Write the child's name and the year below the photo. Laminate or cover with clear self-adhesive paper. The gift is ready to wrap in the hand-shaped wrapping paper.

Super Sledders

Materials

colored construction paper

yarn

child's photo or self-portrait

pencil

scissors

glue

Directions

Students trace closed hand shape onto two pieces of colored construction paper, thumb up on one of the shapes. Cut out. Put the two hand shapes together by gluing fingers to overlap each other. This makes the sled. Add red or some brightly colored piece of yarn to the front of the sled to resemble a rope for pulling. Inside the sled, place a photo or self-portrait of each child to make it look like the child is riding in the hand-shaped sled. For the bulletin board background, use sky blue paper with white at the bottom to resemble snow.

Literature Selection

The Snowy Day
by Ezra Jack Keats
Viking, 1962

Suggested Activity

Have a snow day at school. Tell students in advance and send a note home to advise parents that there will be a snow day at school. (See sample letter on page 48.) On the designated day, bundle up and play outside in the snow for $1/2$ hour to 1 hour in midmorning or early afternoon. Be sure to bring extra coats, boots, mittens, etc., for students who forget. After playing outside, a warm treat could be hot chocolate with marshmallows for all students.

Note

See the letter on page 48 to be used with this activity.

Dear Parents,

We are celebrating the cold weather by having a Play in the Snow Day at school. On this day, please send extra clothes with your child including snowsuits, scarves, mittens, boots and a large plastic bag in which to send wet clothes home. We will be outside for $1/2$ hour to 1 hour during the middle of the day. Parents are welcome to join us or bring sleds to school for students to use.

Our snow day will be _____.

Hope to see you!

Sincerely,

_____ and class

Hands

Materials

white and black con-
    struction paper*
pencil
scissors
glue

Directions

Students should trace hand shape including wrist and arm onto white and black construction paper and cut out. Glue the two hands together to represent the unity between African American people and people of other races. This unity is celebrated in January on Dr. Martin Luther King, Jr.s birthday, due to his involvement in making this unity a reality.

Literature Selections

A Picture Book of Martin Luther King, Jr.
by David A. Adler
Holiday, 1989

Martin Luther King Day
by Linda Lowery
Carolrhoda Books, 1987

Happy Birthday, Martin Luther King
by Jean Marzollo
Scholastic, Inc., 1993

Suggested Activities

Read the literature selections that tell the story of Martin Luther King, Jr. Copy page 50 for each student to color and complete. Students can take this paper home and share with their parents what they have learned about Martin Luther King, Jr.

Note

See page 50 for a worksheet to be used with this activity.

*If you have or can find construction paper in a variety of skin tones, it would be appropriate for this activity. Or you might want to use white paper and color with some of the "multicultural" crayons.

Name: _____

Directions

Draw a picture of something you hope will happen in your life. Then color the page.

Snowflake Person

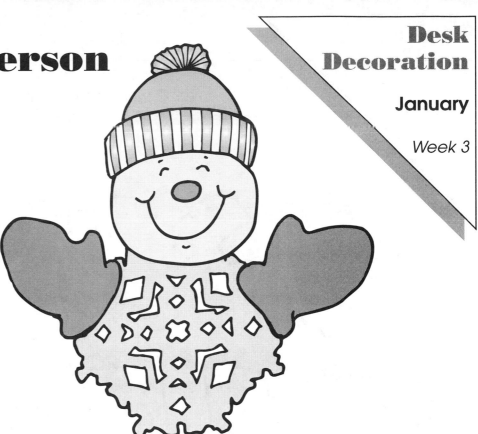

Materials

crayons or markers
construction paper
fabric (optional)
glue glitter or paint, etc.
scissors
glue

Directions

Use the patterns on pages 52-54 to make the snowflake, face and hat. Color the hat and face.

Students should trace their closed hand shapes onto construction paper or fabric and cut out. The hand shapes will be the mittens for the snowflake person.

When all the pieces are cut out, assemble the snowflake person as shown. After assembling, write the student's name through the middle of the snowflake. The name can be written with marker, glue glitter, colored glue, paint, etc.

Literature Selections

The Mitten: A Ukranian Folktale
by Jan Brett
Putnam Publishing Group, 1990

Fun in the Snow
by Laura Damon
Troll Associates, 1988

The Jacket I Wear in the Snow
by Shirley Neitzel
Greenwillow, 1989

A Winter Day
by Douglas Florian
Greenwillow, 1987

Sadie and the Snowman
by Allan Morgan
Scholastic, 1987

Suggested Activity

Read *Frosty the Snowman* to students. Then discuss all things that can be made from snowflakes. Make snow slushes using cups of clean snow with Kool-Aid™.

Note

See pages 53 and 54 for patterns to be used with this activity. Use coloring pattern on page 52 with students who do not wish to cut out their own snowflakes.

Coloring Pattern

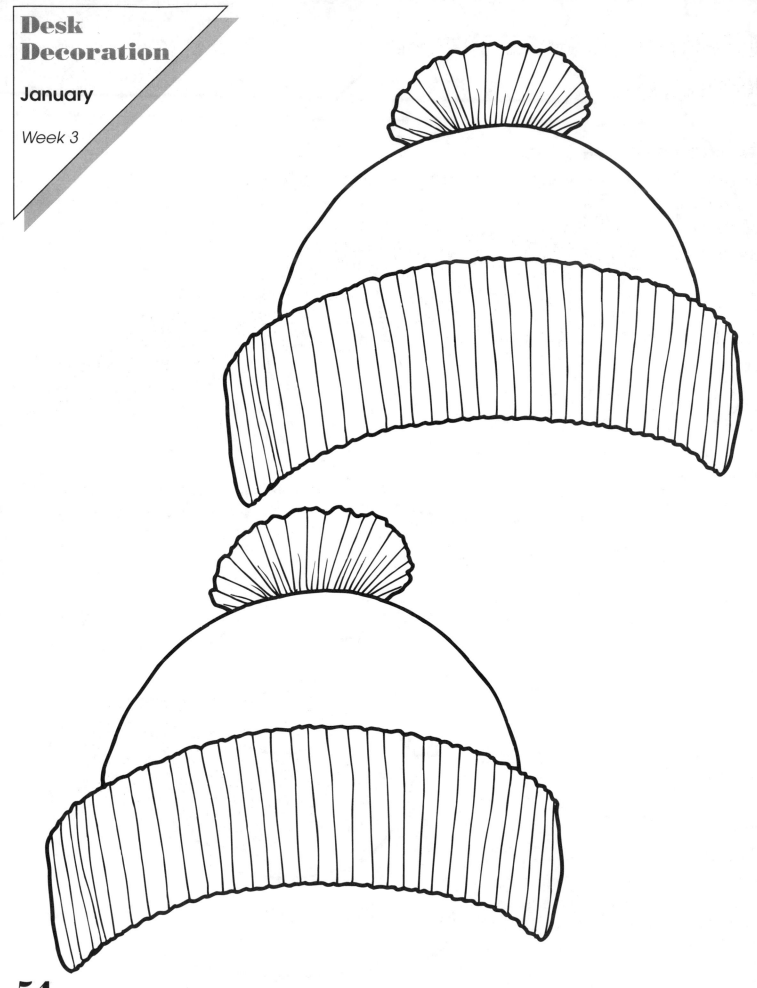

Chinese New Year Dragon

Materials

construction paper, wallpaper scraps, foil paper, paper bags

white paint

shoe boxes

tape

sequins

black marker

yarn

2 Ping-Pong™ or Styrofoam™ balls

Directions

Trace students' hand shapes onto brightly colored construction paper. You can also use wallpaper scraps, foil paper, paper bags that have been flattened and sponge-painted with bright colors or decorated with glue glitter or other decorated paper (comics create an interesting effect, but the paper is thin and difficult for young children to handle without tearing). You will need many, many hand shapes to cover the dragon's head, tail and body sections.

Head

Prepare the shoe box lid as follows:

Place lid upside down and cut one short end and both long sides in a pointed-tooth fashion. Paint the teeth white. Attach the uncut short end to the shoe box with tape. Cover box with hand-shaped scales. Create a mane around the face by folding hand shapes forward. Glue on Ping-Pong™ ball eyes. Draw pupils on the eyes and add a nose with black marker.

Body Sections

Poke holes in the center of the short ends of the boxes. Tie a knot in one length of yarn and pull through the hole from the inside to the outside. Make sure the knot is large enough to hold. Repeat for the other side. Attach the lid to the box with tape. Cover with hand-shaped scales. Make as many body sections as you wish.

Tail

Remove one short end of the shoe box and cut top and bottom as shown.

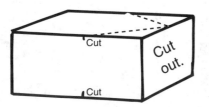

Bring open ends of box together and tape.

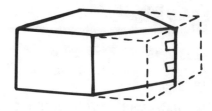

Cover with hand-shaped scales, extend beyond box end.

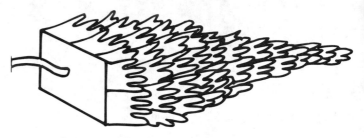

Attach yarn and join to last body section.

If you want to turn this into a larger project, invite the whole school to contribute hand-shaped scales. Cover cardboard boxes large enough for children to wear. Black pants or tights make great dragon legs. Use panty hose eggs for eyes.

Literature Selections

A Dragon Parade: A Chinese New Year Story
by Steven Chin
Raintree (Steck-Vaughn), 1992

Chinese New Year's Dragon
by Rachel Sing
Simon & Schuster, 1994

Valentine Envelopes

Materials

pink or red paper plates
construction paper
stickers, glitter, etc.

Directions

Use two pink or red paper plates. Trace students left and right hand shapes, one onto each plate, enlarging the hand shapes to fill as much of the plate as possible.

Decorate the plates using construction paper, stickers, glitter, fabric, sequins, etc. Write the student's name in large print on each plate so it can be read clearly by other students.

Using the palm as the bottom of the envelope, turn the hand shape plates to face each other so thumbs are together and staple or thread yarn along the bottom and sides. Leave the top open so valentine cards can be put in the top. On Valentine's Day students can use these as their envelopes to exchange valentine cards.

Literature Selections

Will You Be My Valentine?
by Steven Kroll
Holiday, 1993

Arthur's Valentine
by Marc T. Brown
Little, Brown & Co., 1988

Suggested Activity

Frost and decorate valentine (heart shaped) cookies to eat. Depending on time and cooking facilities, you can mix and frost/decorate at school.

Ready-to-use frosting cans/tubes come in a variety of colors and are easy for children to use. Red hots, decorating candies, sprinkle sugar, etc., are fun to put on the cookies after frosting.

Note

See page 58 for recipe to be used with this activity.

Easy Cookie Recipe

2 eggs

^{2}/$_3$ cup (160 ml) shortening

^{2}/$_3$ cup (160 ml) butter or margarine

1^1/$_2$ cups (360 ml) sugar

3^1/$_2$ cups (840 ml) flour

2 tsp. (10 ml) baking powder

1 tsp. (5 ml) salt

2 tsp. (10 ml) vanilla

Beat eggs in large bowl. Add remaining ingredients and blend on low with electric mixer. Mix on medium till well blended. Form a ball. Roll out dough on floured surface and cut into holiday shapes with cookie cutters. Bake at 375°F (190°C) for 8-10 minutes.

Optional:

Frosting

^{1}/$_2$ cup (120 ml) shortening

^{1}/$_2$ cup (120 ml) margarine

1 box powdered sugar (sifted)

1^1/$_2$ tsp. (7.5 ml) vanilla

pinch of salt

1 T. (15 ml) milk

Cream shortening and margarine using electric mixer. Add powdered sugar a little at a time, blending well. Add salt, vanilla, milk. Beat well. More milk can be used to make icing creamier.

58

Valentine Cards

Materials

construction paper

lined paper

glitter, sequins, ribbon,
    stickers, etc.

scissors

glue

Directions

Trace hand shape onto a folded sheet of paper, putting the fold at the bottom of the palm. Cut out hand shape, making sure not to cut on the fold.

Students can decorate/print a message on the front of their hand-shaped card. For younger students, the message can be preprinted or photocopied and glued on the card. Decorate the inside or just write who the valentine goes to and who it is from.

Glitter, construction paper hearts, sequins, ribbon, stickers, etc., can be used to decorate each valentine.

These valentines can be used for classmates, school staff, family members and others.

Literature Selections

The Valentine Bears
by Eve Bunting
Houghton-Mifflin, 1985

The Best Valentine in the World
by Marjorie Weinman Sharmat
Holiday House, 1982

Suggested Activity

If you want to stress proper letter formation during the writing stage of this activity, use lined paper. Then cut and glue the words onto the valentines.

Note

See page 60 for patterns to be used with this activity.

SWEET

Be My Valentine!

Will you be my valentine?

Happy Valentine's Day!

BE MINE

Shadows

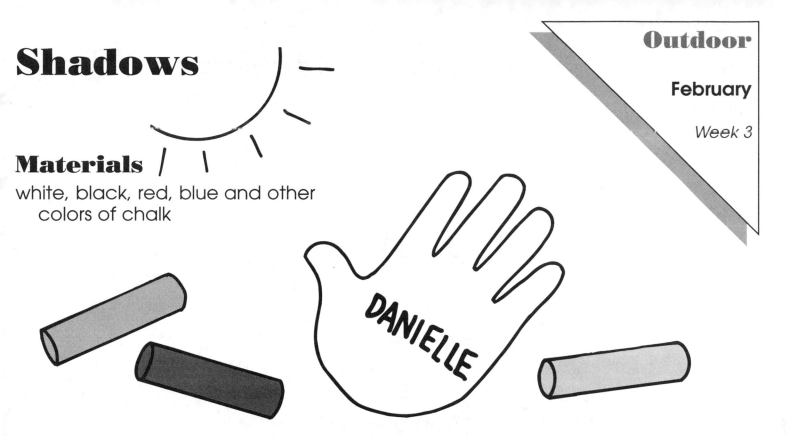

Materials

white, black, red, blue and other
colors of chalk

Directions

Early on a sunny school day in February, have students go outside to the sidewalk, cement play area, etc., and trace around their hands with chalk. Color in the outline with the white chalk. Use this as the "original" handprint. Write student's name on the white hand with black chalk.

After coloring the handprint white, have students put their hand back down directly on top of the white handprint. With red chalk, have students outline the shadow of their handprint.

Later in the morning, before noon, have students go back outside and put their hand directly over the "original" white handprint. This time outline the shadow of their handprint with blue chalk.

Try to repeat this activity at least four times during the school day. Be sure

to use a different color of chalk for each time of the day. Keep track of the time of day each shadow outline is drawn.

If it is warm enough, go outside and discuss the results of your shadow handprints as you look at them. If it is too cold, go back inside and re-create the shadow diagram on the chalkboard. Then discuss how the shadow changed throughout the day.

Let children offer their ideas about why the shadow outline moved as the day progressed. Then explain how the Earth is always moving, thus creating different angles of the sun on the Earth.

Literature Selection

It's Groundhog Day!
by Steven Kroll
Holiday, 1987

Presidents' Day

Materials

paper
pencil
scissors

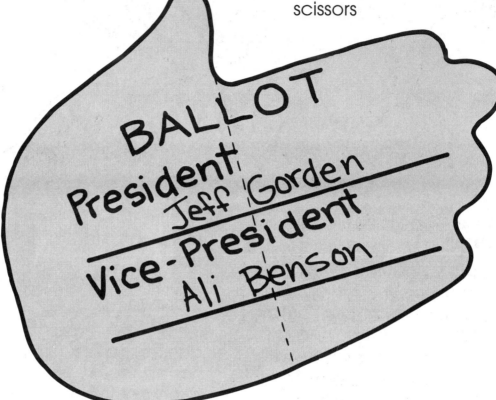

BALLOT
President
Jeff Gorden
Vice-President
Ali Benson

Directions

Select an isolated corner of your classroom or hallway to set up a voting booth. Discuss with students the importance of privacy while casting votes. In the voting booth you need to have paper, pencil and scissors. Students make their own ballot by tracing their hand shape onto paper and it cutting out. On the hand-shaped ballot, students should write the name of the classmate who they want to be class president for a day.

Literature Selections

My First Presidents' Day Book
by Jane B. Moncure
Children's, 1987

The Buck Stops Here, the Presidents of the United States
by Alice Provensen
HarperTrophy, 1990

Suggested Activity

Prior to voting, discuss with the class the duties of class president for a day. These duties can be teacher selected or student selected. For example: Class president can be line leader for a day. Class president can pass out papers for a day. Class president can pick what games to play at recess. Class president can choose one assignment not to do for the day.

Extended Activity

Discuss some of the duties of the President of the United States. Be sure all students know the name of the President of the United States. Talk about some famous Presidents.

Lion and Lamb

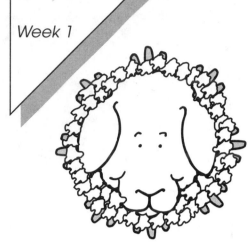

Materials

small paper plates

brown construction paper

white construction paper

cotton balls

scissors

glue

Directions

Lion

Duplicate a lion face pattern (see page 65) for every student. Students can color the lion face and glue it onto a small paper plate.

On brown construction paper, have students trace their open hand shape eight to ten times. Then cut hand shapes out. Glue the palms of the hand shapes to the back of the paper plate to make the lion's mane. Students can curl the paper fingers around a pencil to make the lion's mane circle its face.

Lamb

Duplicate a lamb face pattern (see page 65) for every student. Students can color the lamb face and glue it onto a small paper plate.

On white construction paper, have students trace their open hand shape six to eight times. Then cut hand shapes out. As with the lion, glue palms of hand shapes to the back of the paper plate with the lamb face. Glue cotton balls onto the paper fingers to circle the lamb's face.

Literature Selections

What Will the Weather Be Like Today?
by Paul Rogers
Greenwillow, 1990

A First Discovery Book
by Pascale de Bourgoing
Scholastic, Inc., 1991

Suggested Activity

Discuss with students the adage about March coming "in like a lion . . . out like a lamb."

Then copy the weather chart on page 66 for each student. Help students to note the weather for every school day in March and discuss at the end of the month.

Note

See pages 65 and 66 for patterns to be used with this activity.

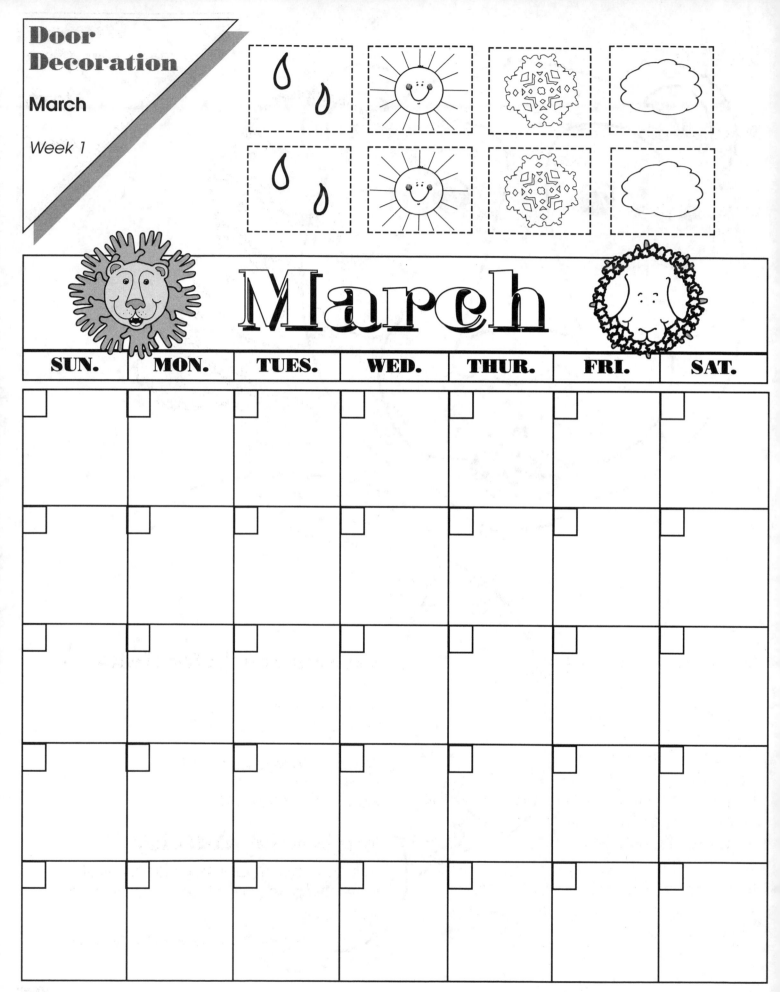

March

SUN.	MON.	TUES.	WED.	THUR.	FRI.	SAT.

Kite

Materials

brightly colored construction
    paper

glitter, fabric, sequins,
    stickers, etc.

yarn

scissors

glue

Directions

Trace hand shape
one time onto four
different colors of
construction paper
and cut out. Glue the hand shapes
together at the palms. Decorate the
hand shapes with glitter, fabric,
sequins, stickers, etc.

Add yarn for a tail. Tie fabric scraps
to the yarn kite tail. Hang these in
the classroom window to welcome
windy March.

Literature Selections

Kites Sail High
by Ruth Heller
Grosset and Dunlap, 1988

Curious George Flies a Kite
by H.A. Rey
Houghton-Mifflin, 1973

Suggested Activity

Encourage students to bring real
kites to school and/or bring kites of
your own.

Enjoy kite flying on a windy day in
March.

Shamrock

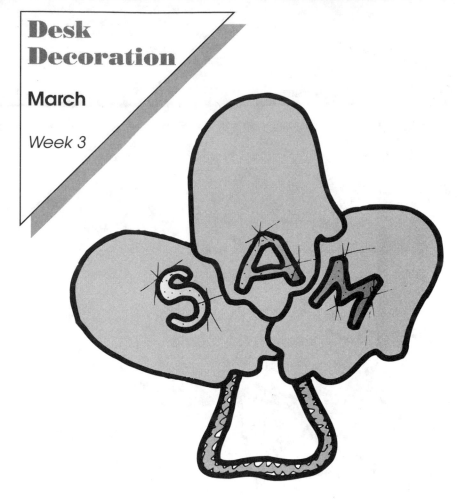

Materials

green construction paper
green pipe cleaner
glitter glue
scissors

Directions

Trace closed handprint three times onto green construction paper and cut out. Glue hand shapes together at the fingers to make a shamrock. Add a green pipe cleaner for a stem. With glitter glue, write student's name across the shamrock.

Use these as name tags for desks. Or use them on a bulletin board by enlarging the pattern on page 69 and putting the shamrocks at the foot of the rainbow.

Literature Selections

Leprechauns Never Lie
by Lorna Balian
Abingdon Press, 1981

Mary McLean and the St. Patrick's Day Parade
by Steven Kroll
Scholastic, Inc., 1993

St. Patrick's Day
by Gail Gibbons
Holiday House, 1994

Suggested Activity

On St. Patrick's Day, encourage everyone in your school to wear green. Then parade through the halls, classrooms and gym to celebrate St. Patrick's Day.

Award a prize in each grade for the person wearing the most green on St. Patrick's Day.

Note

See page 69 for pattern to be used with this activity.

Fingerpaint

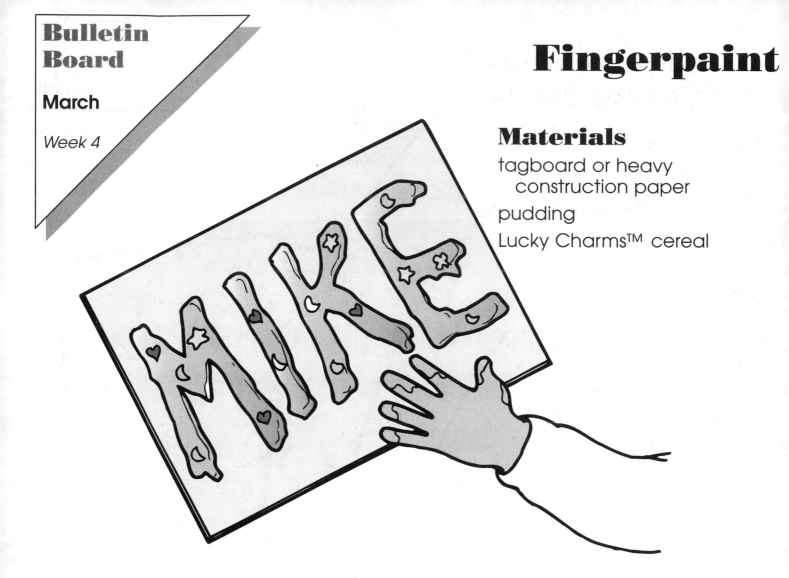

Materials

tagboard or heavy
    construction paper

pudding

Lucky Charms™ cereal

Directions

Use tagboard or sturdy construction paper for pictures. Allow students to dip their hands into individual bowls of pistachio or green-colored vanilla or banana pudding. Then students use their pudding-covered hands to create a picture or write their name onto the tagboard or heavy paper. Add Lucky Charms™ cereal pieces and marshmallow pieces to give the picture a three-dimensional effect.

Literature Selections

Clever Tom and the Leprechaun
by Linda Shute
Lothrop, 1988

A Color of His Own
by Leo Lionni
Knopf, 1993

Suggested Activity

Make Lucky Charms™ cereal bars for children to enjoy after their artwork is finished.

Note

See page 71 for recipe to be used with this activity.

Lucky Charms™ Cereal Bars

¹/4 cup (60 ml) butter or margarine

1 pkg. (10 oz. (283.5 g) about 40)
   regular marshmallows or 4 cups
   (960 ml) miniature marshmallows

5 cups (1 L) Lucky Charms™ cereal

Melt margarine or butter in large
saucepan over low heat.

Add marshmallows and stir until
completely melted.

Cook over low heat three
minutes–stirring constantly.

Remove from heat.

Add Lucky Charms™ cereal.

Stir until well coated.

Press mixture evenly into buttered 9" x
13" (23 x 33 cm) pan.

Cut into squares when cooled.

TLC10028 Copyright © Teaching & Learning Company, Carthage, IL 62321

Showers of Good Work

Materials
blue construction paper
silver glitter glue
scissors

Directions
Trace the individual closed hand-prints of each student onto blue construction paper and cut out. Write the student's name on the palm of the hand, using silver glitter glue. You could also cover each hand shape with plastic wrap or frosted self-adhesive paper to make the raindrops appear shiny and wet. Use the hand-shaped raindrops on a bulletin board entitled "Showers of Good Work." Attach each child's good work to the raindrop with his name on it.

Literature Selections
Big Sarah's Little Boots
by Paulette Bourgeous and Brenda Clark
Scholastic, Inc., 1989

Rain
by Robert Kalan
Greenwillow, 1978

Suggested Activity
Outdoor "Splash" Day

Use a large plastic tub to make bubbles like a bubble bath. Do measuring/predicting activities outdoors using water and measuring cups.

Use the recipe on page 73 to make bubble solution to create giant soap bubbles. With this solution use coat hangers that you have bent into a loop, flyswatters, spatulas, wisk spoons or commercially made giant bubble toys, to make large bubbles.

Note
See page 73 for recipe to use with this activity.

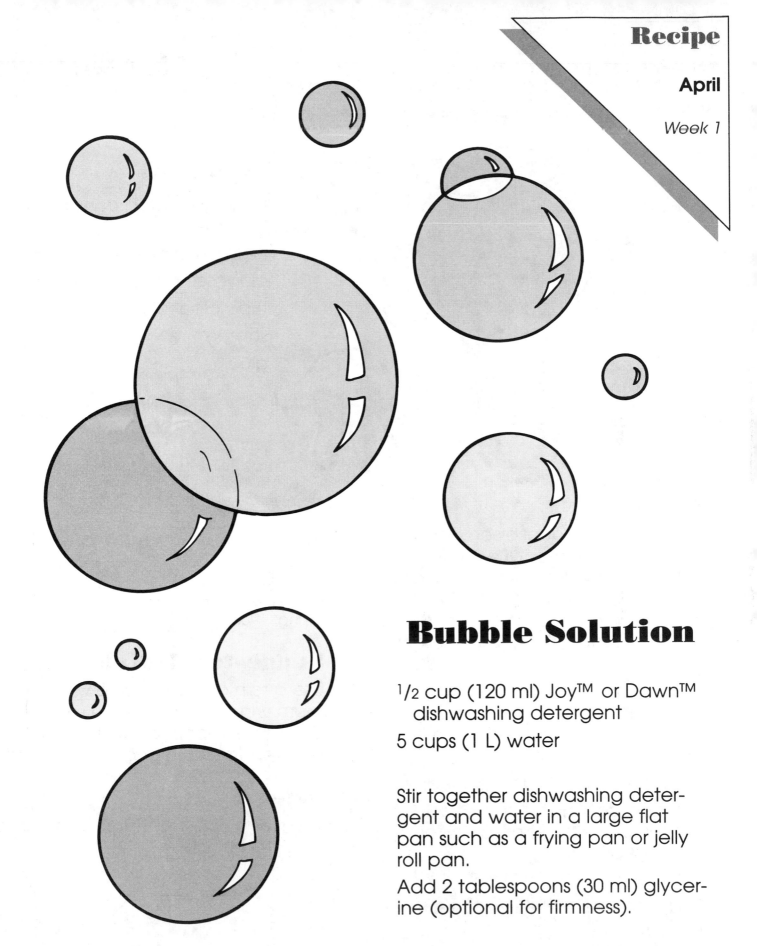

Bubble Solution

1/2 cup (120 ml) Joy™ or Dawn™
    dishwashing detergent

5 cups (1 L) water

Stir together dishwashing deter-
gent and water in a large flat
pan such as a frying pan or jelly
roll pan.

Add 2 tablespoons (30 ml) glycer-
ine (optional for firmness).

Umbrella

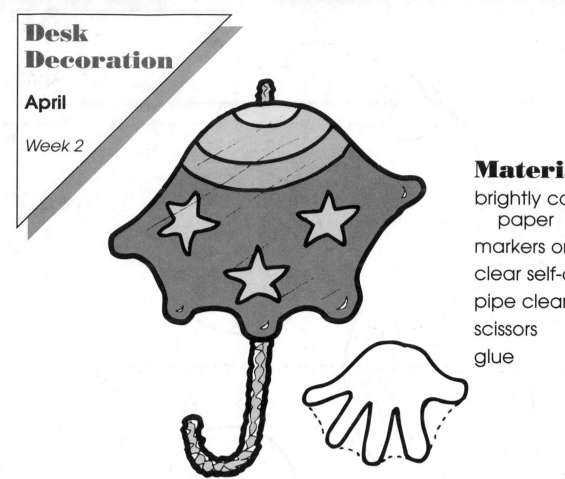

Materials

brightly colored construction paper

markers or crayons

clear self-adhesive paper

pipe cleaners

scissors

glue

Directions

Trace the individual open handprint of every student onto brightly colored construction paper and cut out. Decorate hand-shaped umbrellas using markers or crayons. Be sure to write students' names on umbrellas.

Then laminate umbrellas or cover them with clear self-adhesive paper so that the finish appears shiny and wet.

Add a handle using pipe cleaners.

Use as a desk name tag or add to the raindrops bulletin board for week one of April.

Literature Selections

Rain Talk
by Mary Serfozo
Macmillan, 1990

Thunder Cake
by Patricia Polacco
Putnam Publishing Group, 1990

Umbrella
by Taro Yashima
Viking, 1958

Suggested Activity

Use a rain gauge outside your classroom window to measure rainfall during the month of April. Graph your results at the end of the month.

Note

See page 75 for patterns to be used with this activity.

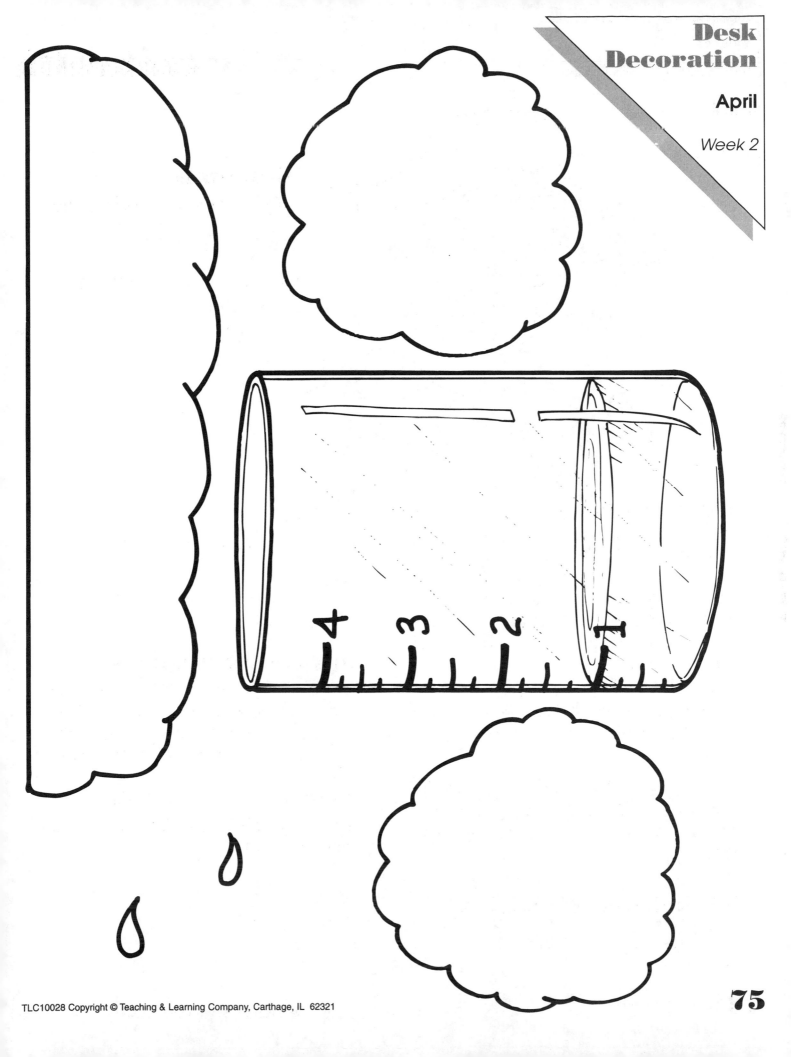

Eggs in a Basket

Materials

pastel-colored construction paper

rickrack, yarn, fabric stickers, sequins, glitter, etc.

scissors

glue

Directions

Trace student's closed handprint onto pastel-colored construction paper and cut out, leaving the thumb off the hand shape. Decorate hand-shaped eggs using rickrack, yarn, fabric, stickers, sequins, glitter, etc. Reproduce the basket pattern on page 78 to glue the eggs into. Color and cut out the basket. Hang baskets full of hand-shaped eggs in the classroom window to decorate for Easter.

Literature Selections

The Egg Tree
by Katherine Milhous
Charles Scribner's Sons, 1971

Chickens Aren't the Only Ones
by Ruth Heller
Grosset and Dunlap, 1981

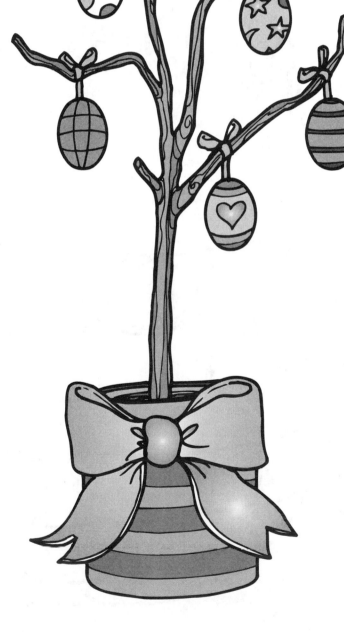

Suggested Activity

Make a classroom egg tree by blowing the contents out of eggs and coloring the eggs in dye. When the eggs have dried, string thread through the holes in each end of the egg. Use the thread to hang the eggs from branches of a small tree or branch that has been secured into a coffee can with sand or cement.

Optional: Use a wax crayon to write student's name on the egg before dyeing so the student can take the egg home for Easter. The best way to get the egg home, is to wrap it in tissue or paper towel and put it in a rinsed-out pint-sized milk carton from the school cafeteria. Then tape the top of the carton down to help secure the egg for the trip home.

Note

See page 78 for pattern to be used with this activity.

Tree

Materials

brown construction paper
soap shavings
green finger paint
scissors
glue

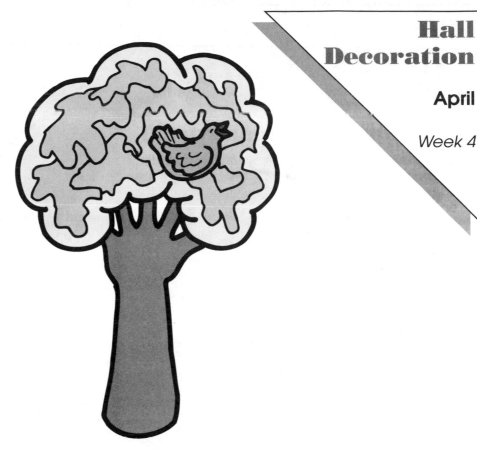

Wake Me in the Spring
by James Preller
Scholastic, Inc., 1994

Directions

Trace individual open hand shapes onto brown construction paper, making sure to include the wrist and arm to the elbow. Then cut out. This is the trunk of the tree. Copy a treetop pattern (see page 80) for each student.

Using soap shavings mixed into green fingerpaint, paint the top of the tree and let dry. Attach the treetop to the hand-shaped trunk and use as a hall decoration.

Optional: Use the bird pattern on page 80 to color and cut out. Then glue the bird into the treetop as a sign of spring.

Literature Selections

The Tree
by Pascale de Bourgoing
Scholastic, Inc., 1992

Suggested Activities

On chart paper, brainstorm a list of all the signs of spring. Then take a walk around the school yard or town to see how many signs of spring your class can find.

When you get back to the classroom, compare signs of spring you actually saw with the list you made.

Add to the list if needed, after the walk.

Note

See page 80 for patterns to be used with this activity.

Grocery Bag Fish Piñata

Materials

brightly colored construction paper

large grocery bag

wrapped candy, stickers and other piñata treats

white construction paper

black marker

scissors

glue

tape

yarn

stapler

(*Use some foil paper if making the "Rainbow Fish.")

Directions

Spread open fingers and trace hand shapes onto brightly colored construction paper. Cut out. Cut out two large (4" (10 cm)) circles for eyes. Open the grocery bag. Place your hands inside the bag and bring the short sides together. Staple closed. This is the head. Position eye circles on either side of the head and glue in place.

Fill paper bag with treats. Gather open end of bag and wrap with tape. This will be the fish's tail. Before you tape the open end, make sure the bag is as puffy as you can make it with the sides as smooth as possible.

Tape or glue hand shapes to the bag, overlapping palms and covering the bag as much as possible. Hang with yarn.

Have children take turns swinging at the piñata until it breaks and the treats are released.

Variation for Young Children

Instead of taping the bag closed, tie it shut with a yarn bow. Hang the fish just high enough so that children must jump to reach an end of the yarn. Whoever can grasp an end will untie the bow and release the treats. (Be sure to hang the fish from something solid and secure.)

Literature Selection

Cinco de Mayo
by Janet Riehecky
Children's, 1993

Rainbow Fish
by Marcus Pfister
North-South Books, 1990

Mother's Day Gift

Materials

construction paper or wallpaper scraps

scissors

glue

These hands bring a promise for Mother's Day;
I'll do my best in every way.
I'll try to make you proud of me
And hope you'll enjoy this cup of tea.

Directions

Trace handprint two times onto construction paper or wallpaper scraps/samples. Cut out the handprints and glue or tape along the bottom and sides to make a pocket for the tea bag.

Copy the poem on page 84 for every student. Then glue the hand-shaped pocket with tea bag inside, to a large piece of tagboard or construction paper. Glue the copied poem next to the hand-shaped pocket. This makes a nice place mat for Mother's Day or a large Mother's Day card.

Literature Selection

The Wednesday Surprise
by Eve Bunting
Clarion Books, 1990

This book will help students remember grandmothers on Mother's Day. It also helps children realize that not all gifts have to be bought in a store.

Suggested Activity

Brainstorm ideas for gifts that students can give to Mom, Dad, grandparents, sister, brother, etc., that do not cost money and are not bought in a store.

For example:
    Help with chores at home
    Kind words

Note

See page 84 for poem to be used with this activity.

These hands bring a promise for Mother's Day;
I'll do my best in every way.
I'll try to make you proud of me
And hope you'll enjoy this cup of tea.

Flower

Materials

brightly colored construction
    paper

green construction paper

scissors

glue

Directions

Trace student's hand shape onto
brightly colored construction paper
and cut out. Reproduce the stem
pattern on page 86 onto green construction paper. Glue the hand-
shaped flower on top of the stem.

Use these hand-shaped flowers to
decorate your classroom window for
spring. Add green construction
paper that has been fringed at the
top as grass for the flowers to
stand in.

Optional: The hand-shaped flowers
and fringe grass could be added to
the hallway along with the hand-
shaped trees (page 79) to make a
spring mural.

Literature Selection

Queen of the May
by Steven Kroll
Holiday, 1993

Suggested Activity

Use a pole on the playground to create a Maypole. Hang brightly colored streamers from the top of the
pole. Be sure there is one streamer
for every student and teacher in
your class. During the afternoon, go
outside and dance around the
Maypole.

Discuss with your class the origin of
May Day and the Maypole.

Note

See page 86 for pattern to be used
with this activity.

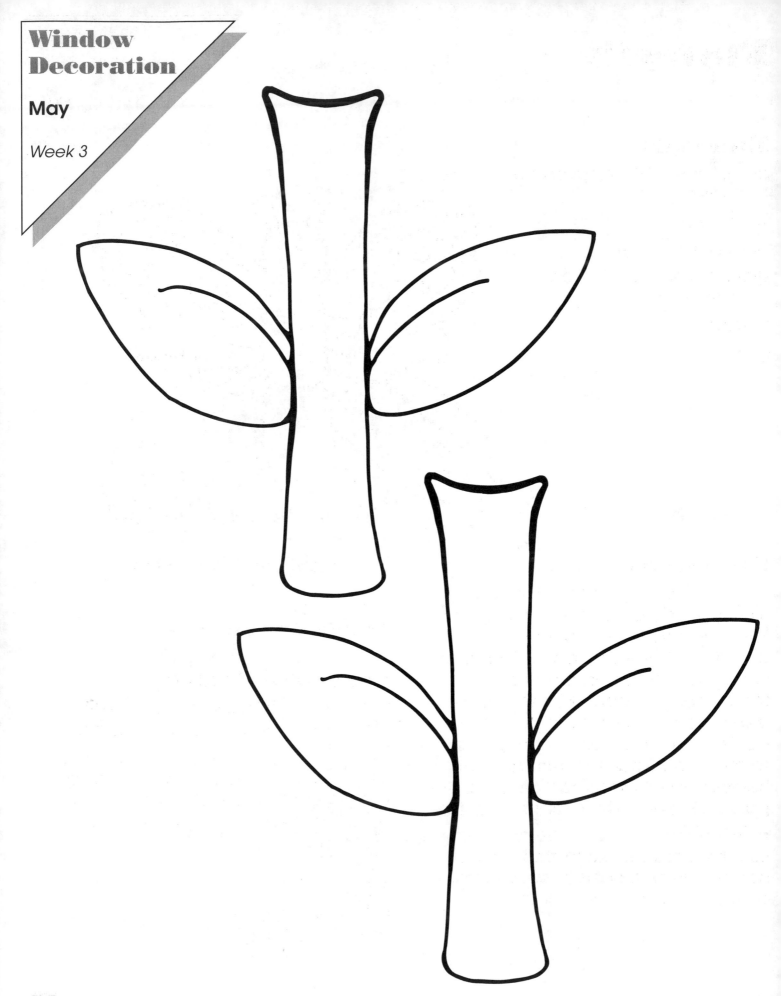

Butterfly

Materials

pastel or brightly colored construction paper

wiggly eyes

pom-pom

stickers, yarn, fabric, sequins, glitter, etc.

scissors

glue

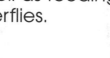

Directions

Trace student's closed hand shape four times onto pastel or brightly colored construction paper and cut out. Attach the four palms together with glue. Then add the body from the pattern on page 88. The body can be colored and wiggly eyes added with a tiny pom-pom glued to the end of each antennae. The hand-shaped wings can be decorated with stickers, yarn, fabric, sequins, glitter, etc.

Use these butterflies to add to your hand-shaped flowers in the window of your classroom or hallway.

Literature Selection

The Very Hungry Caterpillar
by Eric Carle
Putnam Publishing Group, 1981

Suggested Activity

Use a viewing box kit to observe the process of larvae becoming butterflies.

Kits provide instructions and information on each stage of development, as well as feeding supplies for the butterflies.

Note

See page 88 for pattern to be used with this activity.

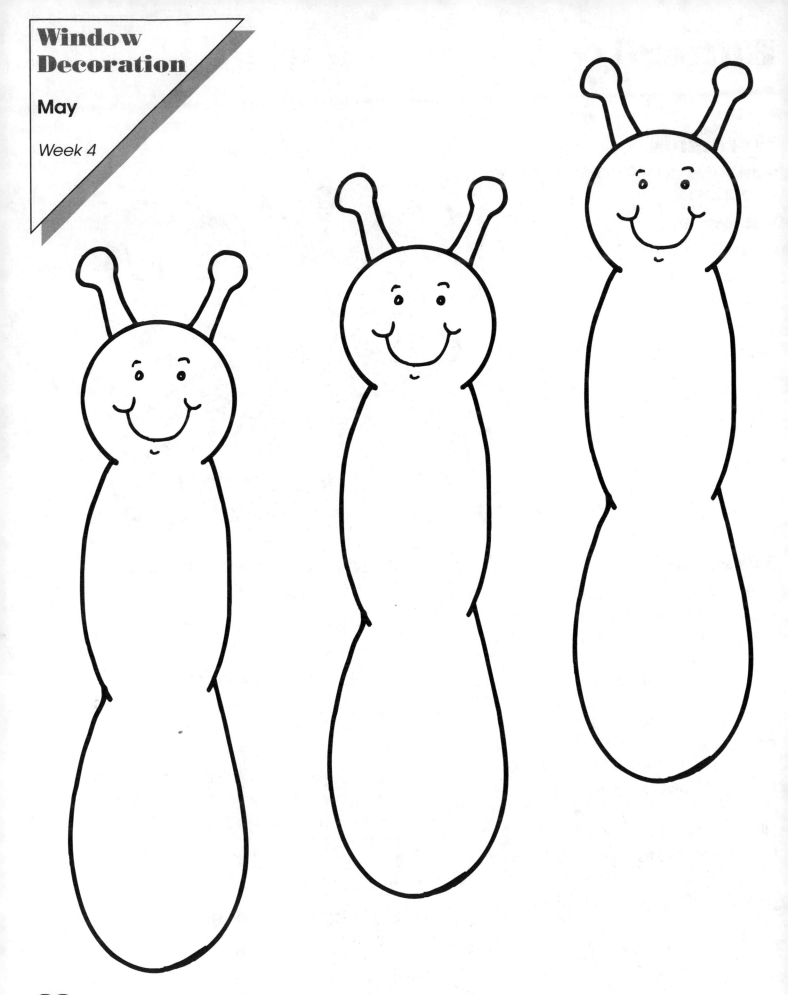

This Is a "Berry" Special Class

Materials

red construction paper
green felt
black paint
paintbrushes

Directions

Trace individual closed handprints of every student onto red construction paper. Cut stem (see pattern on page 90) out of green felt to put at the top of every berry. Use paintbrushes dipped in black to make spots to represent seeds.

For lettering, use red construction paper with black dots painted on it.

Literature Selections

The Little Mouse, the Red Ripe Strawberry and the Big Hungry Bear
by Don and Audrey Wood
Child's Play (International) Ltd., 1990

Strawberry
by Jennifer Coldery and George Bernard
Silver Burdett Press, 1988

Before introducing this door decoration, read the literature selections to familiarize students with strawberries and their appearance.

Suggested Activity

When reading the Woods' selection, do NOT read the ending. Stop reading just prior to the end. Have students draw on paper what they think the mouse in the story will do with the strawberry. After students share their predictions about the end of the story, then read the actual ending in the book. Discuss how students' predictions compare to the authors' ending.

Note

See page 90 for pattern to be used with this activity.

Notepad for Father's Day

Materials

white or colored typing paper
colored construction paper
scissors
stapler

I love Dad!
Happy
Father's Day!

Directions

Students should trace their hand shape onto colored or white typing paper 10 to 20 times and cut out. Also trace hand shape one time onto colored construction paper. On the construction paper hand, help students write:

I Love Dad!   Happy Father's Day!

Put all the hand shapes together with the construction paper hand on top and staple or spiral bind at the palm. This will give Dad a "hand"y notepad to use and a "hand"y reminder that he is loved on Father's Day and always.

Literature Selections

Just Me and My Dad
by Mercer Mayer
Golden Books, 1977

Something from Nothing
by Phoebe Gilman
Scholastic, Inc., 1993

What Is a Family?
by Gretchen Super
Twenty-First Century Books
A Division of Henry Holt and Co., 1991

Suggested Activity

Make gift coupons to give to Dad on Father's Day. Coupons can be redeemed for help with chores around the house or for small favors Dad might appreciate.

For example:
    Rake the yard
    Sweep the garage
    Clean out the car
    Rub or scratch Dad's back

Note

See page 92 for coupons to be used with this activity.

This coupon entitles Dad to

_____

Happy Father's Day!

Love, _____

This coupon entitles Dad to

_____

Happy Father's Day!

Love, _____

This coupon entitles Dad to

_____

Happy Father's Day!

Love, _____

Fireworks

Materials

red, white and blue
   construction paper
silver or gold glitter

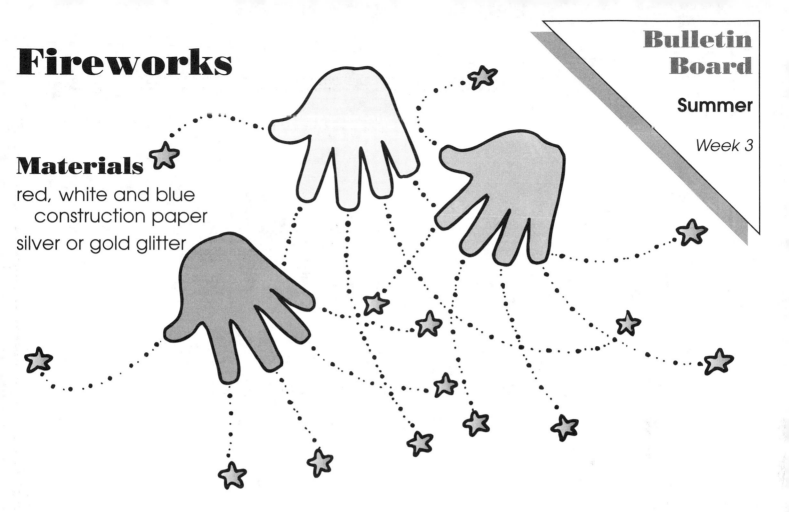

Directions

Students trace open hand shape
onto red, white and blue construction paper and cut out. Staple or
glue these onto white bulletin board
paper or large white construction
paper.

Use silver or gold glitter glued in lines
coming down from each finger of
the hand-shaped fireworks.

This can be used as a July bulletin
board or a picture to be taken
home.

Literature Selections

Stars and Stripes: Our National Flag
by Leonard Everett Fisher
Holiday House, 1993

Star-Spangled Banner
by Peter Spier
Doubleday, 1973

Suggested Activity

Teach students the words to the
United States' national anthem.

Discuss the importance of respect for
the flag and what the flag symbol-
izes for the United States.

Discuss safety as it relates to using
fireworks, sparklers, etc., around the
Fourth of July.

Note

See page 94 for a copy of the words
to the United States national
anthem.

The Star-Spangled Banner

Oh, say can you see by the dawn's early light

What so proudly we hail'd at the twilight's last gleaming,

Whose broad stripes and bright stars through the
perilous fight

O'er the ramparts we watch'd were so gallantly
streaming?

And the rockets' red glare, the bombs bursting in air,

Gave proof through the night that our flag was still there.

Oh, say does that star-spangled banner yet wave

O'er the land of the free and the home of the brave?

by Francis Scott Key

Splash in for a Great Summer

Materials

blue construction paper

student photos or pictures

Directions

Students should trace their closed hand shapes five to six times onto blue construction paper and cut out. Overlap the hand shapes onto your bulletin board to resemble waves of water. Use student photos or self-portraits positioned behind the hand-shaped waves to look like students are swimming in the water.

Entitle the bulletin board "Splash in for a Great Summer."

Literature Selections

Albie the Lifeguard
by Louise Bordon
Scholastic, Inc., 1993

The Magic String
by Francene Sabin
Troll Associates, 1981

Suggested Activity

Discuss swimming safety rules:

Never swim alone.

Learn to swim before going off the diving board or entering water that is over your head.

Do not run at the pool.

Don't push people into the water or hold them under.

Plan a pool party for your class or the entire school. Rent the public pool for two hours in the afternoon or schedule an evening. Use the letter on page 96 to get parental permission for students to attend the pool party.

Note

See page 96 for letter to be used with this activity.

Dear Parents:

Our class will be hosting a pool party on _____,

at _____ p.m.

Please send a swimming suit, towel, sun block, pool toys, etc., to school with your child on this day.

There will be lifeguard supervision during our pool party. However, please reinforce with your child the importance of taking safety precautions around the water. We also welcome any parents who would like to come and help chaperone the event.

You will need to sign the permission slip below to allow your child to attend the pool party.

Thank you!

_____ has my permission to attend

the school pool party on _____.

_____
parent's signature

Happy Birthday

Materials

construction paper
stickers, fabric, sequins, yarn, etc.
crayons
scissors
glue

Directions

Use the pattern on page 99 for students to color and decorate on their birthday. After coloring and decorating, have students put the palm of their hand on the cake and trace their fingers to make enough candles for their age. The finger-shaped candles can be topped with glitter or yellow/orange crayon to make them appear lit.

Jan.	Feb.	Mar.	Apr.	May	Jun.	Jul.	Aug.	Sep.	Oct.	Nov.	Dec.

Debbie, Beth, Dan, Eric (Jan.)
Billy, Briana (Feb.)
Cindi, Jose, Blake (Apr.)
Kassi (May)
Dona, Jeff (Jun.)
Ann (being placed)

Suggested Activity

Make a graph of the months of the year. Have students place a mini birthday cake, with their name and birth date on it, on the graph under the month to show their birthday.

Discuss the completed graph pointing out what month has the most birthdays, the least birthdays, two people who have the same birthday, etc.

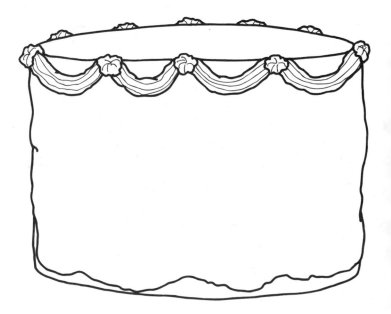

98

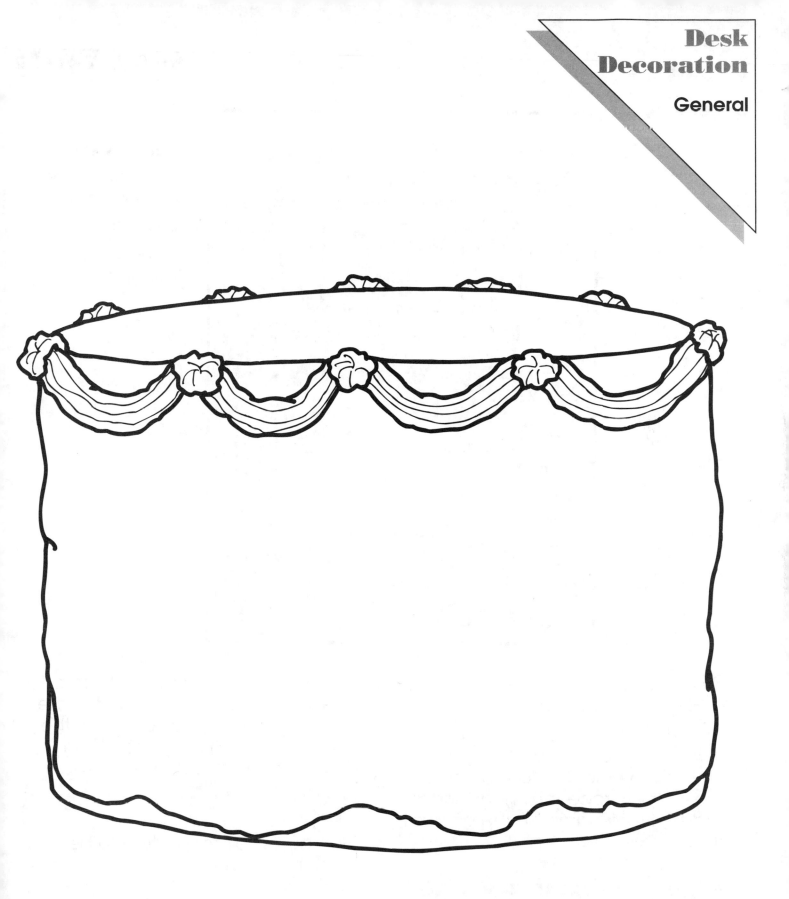

Get Well

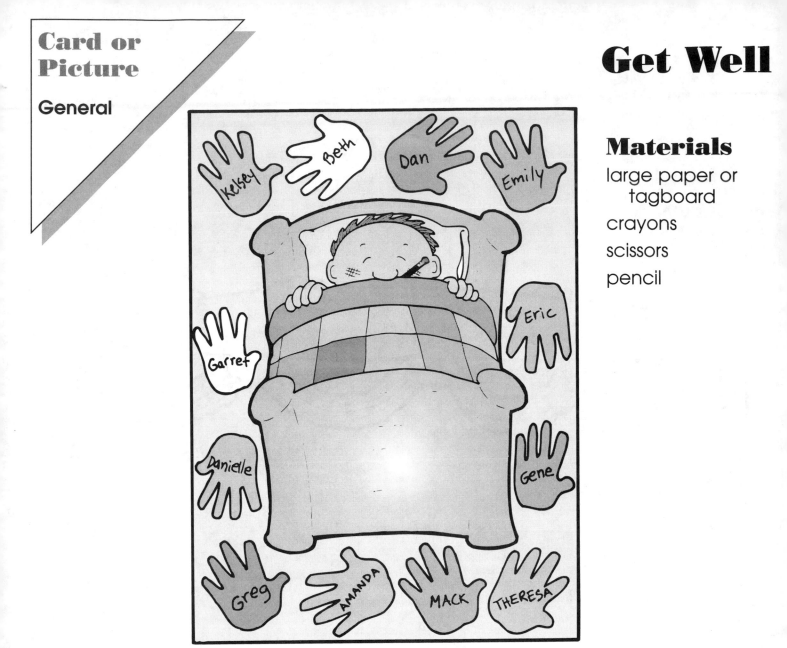

Materials

large paper or
tagboard

crayons

scissors

pencil

Directions

Reproduce the picture of a person
sick in bed on page 101 onto a large
sheet of paper or tagboard. Allow
students to color portions of the picture as they trace their hand shape
and sign their name on the get well
card.

Suggested Activity

Assign one student helper in the
class to take care of getting assign-
ments for that day to send home to
the sick student. At the end of the
day, go over the material with the
student helper to be sure all the
homework is included.

Note

See page 101 for pattern to be used
with this activity.

Welcome

Materials

cardboard or tagboard
construction paper
scissors
glue

Directions

Reproduce the happy face pattern on page 103 onto cardboard or tagboard. Have students trace their hand shape onto different colors of construction paper and cut out. Then students write their name on their paper hand shape and glue to the back side around the happy face.

This will serve as a welcome card for a new student, a guest speaker or visitor to the classroom.

Suggested Activity

This can also serve as a farewell card for a student who has to move away during the school year. You might want to throw a little farewell party and present the card to the student during the party. This will give him something to keep and help remember the class.

Note

See page 103 for pattern to be used with this activity.

Thank-You

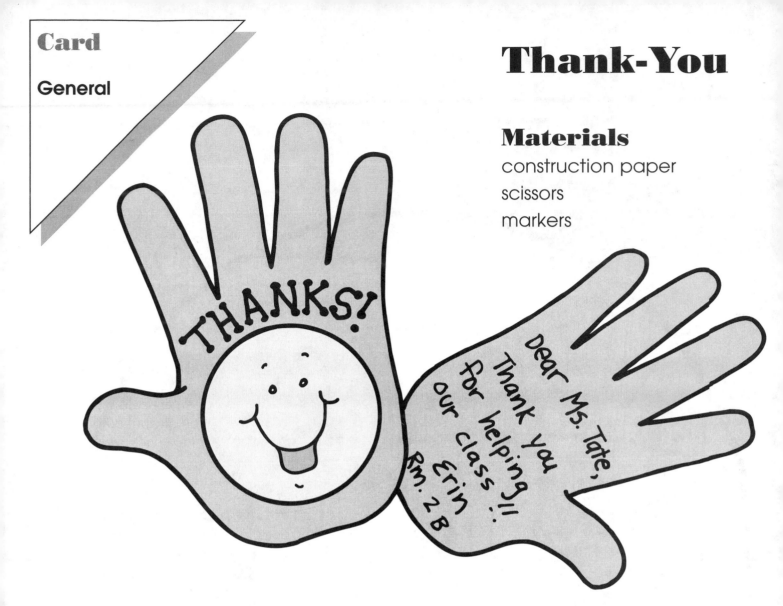

Materials

construction paper
scissors
markers

Directions

Students should trace their hand shape onto different colors of construction paper and cut out. Then use markers to draw a happy face on one side of the paper hand shape. On the other side of the hand shape students can write their own personal thank-you message or copy one the class or teacher has created to fit the occasion.

Suggested Activity

Use a book binder or heavy-duty stapler to fasten all the hand-shaped thank-you cards together. Then send the thank-you cards to someone who has done something nice for your class.

For example:

Parents who volunteer to help at parties, field trips, etc.

Places the class goes to tour

Bus drivers for class trips

Guest speakers who visit the class